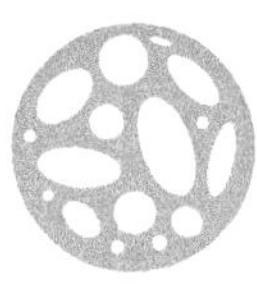

THE SECULAR PATH TO WELL-BEING

Practical Dharma for today

Jeffrey Fracher's 'The Secular Path to Well-Being' gently shows us how to meet life as it is – with presence, compassion, and openness. Blending Buddhist wisdom with modern psychology, he offers a clear path out of habitual reactivity and toward a response of grace. A powerful invitation to step into awakeness, heart-centeredness, and the heart of who we are.

> – Caverly Morgan, author of *A Kids Book About Mindfulness* and *The Heart of Who We Are: Realizing Freedom Together*

'The Secular Path to Well-Being' is a thorough and well written presentation of the beneficial meeting of psychology and secular dharma. Using examples from his own life, Fracher shows how the ancient teachings and practices of the Buddha can greatly enhance a mindful and compassionate life in modern times.

> – Martine Batchelor, author of *Meditation for Life* and *The Spirit of the Buddha*

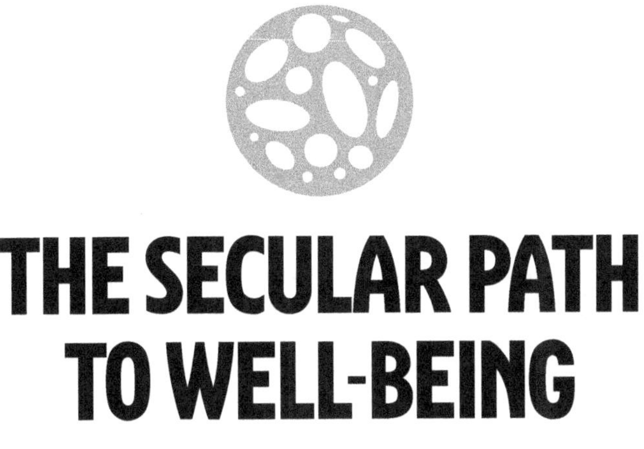

THE SECULAR PATH TO WELL-BEING

Practical Dharma for today

Jeffrey Fracher

First published in 2026 by

Tuwhiri USA
701 Ozier Drive, Batavia, IL 60510, USA
and The Tuwhiri Project Ltd
13 Leith Street, Gisborne 4010, Aotearoa New Zealand

www.tuwhiri.org

ISBN 979-8-9909491-4-0 (Paperback),
ISBN 979-8-9909491-5-7 (Ebook ePub)

US Library of Congress Control Number: 2026902654

A catalogue record for this book is available from the
National Library of New Zealand.
Kei tei pātengi raraunga o Te Puna Mātauranga o Aotearoa
te whakarārangi o tēnei pukapuka.

Support from the Secular Buddhist Association's Secular Buddhist Book
Project, a 501(c)(3) initiative, and Aotearoa Buddhist Education Trust,
are integral to all books published by Tuwhiri. The publishers gratefully
acknowledge this support.

Edited by Ramsey Margolis, with Cathryn Jacob and Winton Higgins
Book design by Ramsey Margolis and John Houston
Cover by minimum graphics
Cover photo by Alexander Milo on Unsplash
Author photograph by Melody Robbins Photography

Set in IBM Plex Serif and Fira Sans
Printed in Aotearoa New Zealand by YourBooks
and in other countries by IngramSpark

Dedication

To my beloved, Kay, for the gift of her in my life

To my boys, Eli and Luke, my pride and joy

To all my students, and the members of Serenity Sangha
*   – my best teachers*

And, finally, to my teacher, Lila Kate Wheeler, who has been
*   my perfect guide*

CONTENTS

Preface   ix

I Experience life   **1**

   1. Introduction   3

   2. Understanding suffering   9

   3. Impermanence and change   19

   4. Ego and self-identity   27

II Let reactivity be   **33**

   5. Reactivity and shame   35

   6. Desire and craving   43

   7. Anger and ill will   49

   8. Anxiety   55

   9. Cultivating patience   65

   10. Judging and comparison   71

III See reactivity stop   **77**

   11. Why we practice the dharma   79

   12. Noticing and mindful awareness   85

   13. Finding calm in overwhelm   91

IV Actualize a path   **99**

   14. Ethics and appropriate living   101

   15. Mindfulness and meditation practice   107

   16. Integrating the path   115

V Human flourishing   **119**

   17. Gratitude and contentment   121

   18. Wise hope and faith   125

VI Relationships   **131**

    19. Relationships: connection and impermanence   133

    20. Healthy boundaries   147

    21. Acceptance and letting go   155

    22. Regret and forgiveness   163

VII Death and grieving   **169**

    23. Facing death   171

    24. Grief and acceptance   177

Afterword   **183**

About the author   **187**

Acknowledgements   **189**

Sources of wisdom   **191**

Index   **195**

Taking the next step   **198**

Preface

The four tasks framework

The origin of the conflict, frustration, and anxiety we experience does not lie in the nature of the world itself but in our distorted conceptions of the world.

Stephen Batchelor

This book represents a synthesis of fundamental teachings from ancient Buddhist wisdom, unencumbered by the supernatural and metaphysical vestiges of the Buddha's time, and modern, evidence-based psychology. Though originating centuries apart, the convergence of the two schools of thought is striking, though not surprising. I consider Gotama, the Buddha, to be the greatest psychologist to ever live, given his brilliant insights into the human psyche and the challenges of being human. The combination of a secular Buddhist perspective with modern psychological theory are what I call 'practical dharma'.

Stephen Batchelor, a prominent contemporary Buddhist teacher and writer, offers a refreshing and pragmatic approach to the dharma through his concept of the four tasks. Instead of basing the dharma on the four noble truths, Batchelor reclaims these ancient teachings as actionable steps that focus on how to live skillfully in the modern world. His approach is not a reinterpretation of Buddhist philosophy. It is a call to engage directly with our lived experience in a way that is grounded, practical, and deeply transformative. The four tasks are foundational to understanding a secular approach to Buddhism.

This book does not offer an exhaustive exploration of Batchelor's four tasks. Nor is it a theoretical exploration of Buddhism or an in-depth examination of modern psychology. Rather it offers a series of pragmatic strategies for incorporating each of the four tasks into our daily lives, informed by psychology. While it is organized sequentially, the implementation of the strategies in each section is not a linear process. Instead, they offer an interactive means of achieving a dramatic shift in how we live our lives day-to-day in way that is consistent with the original intent of Gotama's teachings, shorn of the supernatural and metaphysical 'add-ons'. For a more exhaustive exploration of the four tasks, which is beyond the scope of this book, I recommend Stephen Batchelor's book, *Buddha, Socrates, and Us*.

Batchelor's four tasks – experiencing all of life, letting go of craving, aversion, and delusion-the three poisons-seeing its cessation, and actualizing a path – emphasize action over belief. Rather than ontological truths to be accepted, Batchelor suggests that what have come to be known as the Four Noble Truths are tasks to be performed. This active, process-oriented perspective makes his model particularly relevant for us as we navigate the complexities of contemporary life, where issues such as stress, disconnection, and existential uncertainty often dominate – issues with which modern clinical psychology is also concerned.

In what follows, we will explore these four tasks and examine how they can be broadly applied to the challenges of daily life. By grounding these profound teachings in practical wisdom, we can discover how to live more fully, mindfully, and compassionately.

While Stephen Batchelor's four tasks are rooted in Gotama's teachings they shift the focus from metaphysical claims to pragmatic guidance. They are:

- ✦ **Experience life:** Fully acknowledge the presence of the whole of our life, including suffering, without denial or avoidance.
- ✦ **Let reactivity be:** Understand that craving – our habitual clinging to desires and aversions – is a source of suffering, and practice releasing it.
- ✦ **See reactivity stop:** Cultivate the experience of freedom and peace that arises when craving is absent.
- ✦ **Actualize a path:** Actively engage in practices that foster ethical conduct, mindfulness, and wisdom to sustain this liberation.

Batchelor's reframing transforms the four noble truths from abstract doctrines into a practical guide for living with an emphasis on enacting them in daily life. This shift invites us to engage with the dharma as a process of inquiry and experimentation rather than as a set of fixed dogmas, a shift consistent with evidence-based psychology.

The first task, addressed in section one, **Experience life**, calls on us to fully embrace the reality of suffering. In traditional Buddhist teachings, dukkha is often translated as suffering, but it can also mean unsatisfactoriness, stress, or the inherent instability of life. This task is not about wallowing in negativity or becoming overwhelmed by pain. Instead, it is an invitation to turn toward life's challenges with openness and curiosity.

In our modern lives, we are often conditioned to avoid suffering at all costs. Whether through constant busyness, consumerism or distraction, we seek to escape discomfort rather than face it. However, this avoidance only amplifies our suffering, as we remain trapped in patterns of denial and reactivity.

To embrace life means to acknowledge its presence without resistance. For example, when we experience anxiety or sadness, our habitual response might be to suppress these feelings or distract ourselves. But the first task encourages us to pause, take a breath, and observe what is happening within us. What does anxiety feel like in the body? What thoughts and emotions are arising? By staying present with our experience, we begin to see suffering not as an enemy to be defeated but as a normal part of life that can teach us profound lessons.

This practice of embracing suffering is deeply connected to mindfulness. By cultivating present moment awareness, we slowly develop the capacity to hold both joy and pain with equanimity. Over time, this openness allows us to respond to life's challenges with greater wisdom and compassion.

The second task in section two, **Let reactivity be**, invites us to let go of the habitual grasping that underlies much of our suffering. In Buddhist terms, reactivity is a response to the insatiable desire for things to be different than they are – whether through clinging to pleasure, avoiding pain, or seeking a fixed sense of self.

In today's world, craving is perpetuated by a culture of constant consumption and comparison. Advertisements promise happiness through material possessions, social media fuels envy and insecurity, and the pressure to achieve often leaves us feeling inadequate. This relentless pursuit of more keeps us trapped in a cycle of dissatisfaction. Letting go of reactivity and clinging does not mean suppressing our desires or pretending that we are indifferent to life's pleasures. It involves recognizing the futility of seeking lasting happiness in things that are impermanent. This struggle enables us to understand the nature of desires and the impermanent world in which they arise.

For example, consider the experience of buying a new gadget or item of clothing. At first, we might feel a sense of excitement, but this feeling soon fades, leaving us wanting something else. By observing this pattern, we can begin to loosen our attachment to fleeting pleasures and turn our attention toward deeper sources of fulfillment.

Practically speaking, letting go of craving requires mindfulness and self-inquiry. When we notice ourselves grasping for something – whether it's a new possession, a relationship, or a particular outcome – we can pause and ask: What am I really seeking? Is this craving bringing me closer to peace or further away from it? This process of reflection helps us to let go of the habits that no longer serve us and reconnect with what truly matters.

The third task, section three, **See reactivity stop**, is to recognize and cultivate the cessation of craving which enables us to experience moments of freedom and peace. This is not an abstract or mystical state but rather a tangible experience that arises when we release our grasping and rest in the present moment.

Imagine, for instance, the relief that comes from letting go of a long-held grudge. When we stop clinging to anger and resentment, we feel lighter, freer, and more at ease. Similarly, when we let go of the need to control every aspect of our lives, we open ourselves to the possibility of joy and spontaneity. These moments of release demonstrate that freedom is always available, even in the midst of life's challenges.

To cultivate the cessation of reactivity, we practice mindfulness and meditation. Through these practices, we learn to observe our thoughts and emotions without becoming entangled in them. Over time, we develop the skill of letting be, allowing our experience to unfold without interference. This attitude of non-grasping creates the conditions for peace to arise naturally.

It is important to note that the cessation of reactivity is an ongoing process, not a permanent state. Freedom arises and passes away, just like all other phenomena. By appreciating these moments of release, however fleeting, we deepen our understanding of what it means to live with ease and contentment.

The fourth task, section four, **Actualize a path**, is to develop a way of life that supports the ongoing practice of embracing life, letting go of reactivity, and experiencing the cessation of reactivity. For most ancestral Buddhists, this path is outlined in an eightfold path, which encompasses ethical conduct, mental discipline, and wisdom. Batchelor, however, encourages us to adapt this framework to our unique circumstances and needs, internal and external.

At its core, the path is about living intentionally. It's about aligning our actions, thoughts, and relationships with our deepest values. This requires a commitment to ongoing self-reflection and growth. For example, we might ask ourselves: How can I bring more mindfulness into my daily routines? How can I cultivate kindness and compassion in my interactions with others? How can I create a life that is meaningful and fulfilling?

Cultivating a path might involve establishing a regular meditation practice, engaging in acts of service, and seeking out supportive communities. It might also involve setting boundaries, simplifying our lives, or pursuing creative endeavors, all of which we will cover in later chapters. The key is to find practices that resonate with us personally and that foster a sense of connection, purpose, and well-being.

Importantly, the path is a dynamic process, not a fixed destination. As we walk the path, we will inevitably encounter obstacles and setbacks. But these challenges are not failures; they are opportunities to deepen our practice and refine our understanding. By approaching the path with patience and humility, we can learn to navigate life's ups and downs with greater resilience and grace.

The beauty of Stephen Batchelor's four tasks lies in their practicality. These principles are not confined to the meditation cushion or the retreat center; they are meant to be lived in the messy, complex reality of everyday life. By applying ourselves to the four tasks, we transform everyday challenges into opportunities for growth and awakening. We learn to navigate life's complexities with greater clarity, compassion, and wisdom.

Batchelor's four tasks offer a profound yet accessible framework for living the dharma in the modern world. By shifting the focus from abstract truths to practical tasks, Batchelor invites us to engage with the dharma as a living tradition – one that evolves in response to the needs and challenges of our time.

The four tasks remind us that the path to freedom is not about escaping from life but embracing it fully. It is about meeting suffering with courage, letting go of what binds us, and cultivating a way of life that is rooted in mindfulness, compassion, and wisdom. Above all, it is about discovering the possibility of freedom – right here, in the midst of our ordinary, imperfect lives.

In a world that often feels chaotic and overwhelming, these teachings offer a beacon of hope as well as guidance. They remind us that peace is not something we need to attain; it is something we can uncover, moment by moment, through the simple yet profound act of embodying the four tasks. By committing to this practice, we can transform our lives and contribute to a more compassionate and harmonious world. I welcome you.

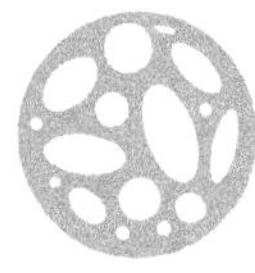

1 • EXPERIENCE LIFE

In this section, we address the realities of the human journey
that are immutable; only by understanding and attempting to
accept these realities, will we make progress on the path

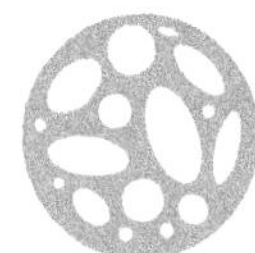

1. Introduction

The seed of suffering in you may be strong, but don't wait until you have no more suffering before allowing yourself to be happy.
   Thich Nhat Hanh

Every one of us experiences suffering. It's a fundamental life experience. The observation about human suffering represents an honest assessment of what it means to be human. People experience distress from various life events which include loss, illness, aging, disappointment and uncertainty. Suffering represents only a part of what life brings to us. In addition to suffering, the human experience also contains joyful and connected moments, as well as times of wonder. The essential task becomes learning to handle suffering while maintaining a purposeful existence.

I left the faith tradition in which I was raised as an adolescent for a number of reasons, none the least of which was the rigid, rule-bound nature of the institution. Though I was raised in a liberal protestant denomination, there were still creeds, concepts, and beliefs, many of which were metaphysical truth claims to which one had to adhere. These supernatural beliefs were simply a bridge too far for me.

What has worked in my own life is the concept of secular spirituality, specifically, secular Buddhism. This involves embracing the benefits of spiritual practices – such as awe, ethics, contemplation, love, wisdom, and community – without adhering to metaphysical truth claims, esoteric convictions, or dogma. In this way, we reject aspects of religion such as dogmatic certainty, while retaining its beneficial elements, including ethical and moral guidance, humility, care for and service to others, and cultural practices, all of which have existed for millennia. We create meaningful lives without compromising rationality or accepting what we feel to be incredible, impossible to believe. Doing so provides access to many of the benefits traditionally associated with religion, such as greater happiness, longevity, better relationships, reduced harmful behaviors, and a sense of community. A personal spiritual practice rooted in authenticity and sustained, thanks to core values, but without the supernatural, offers a sustainable path to inner peace and wholeness.

Stephen Batchelor and other secular Buddhist thinkers present a practical approach to Buddhism which draws from universal human experiences while avoiding metaphysical beliefs. In his writings, Batchelor's focus is on secular Buddhism as a practical philosophy for living one's life. With its emphasis on relying on the dharma to confront the problems of modern living, this is the very reason why I call what I teach practical dharma. The practice of secular Buddhism focuses on developing a lifestyle which enables us to handle life's difficulties through enhanced wisdom and compassion, and clear understanding. As Winton Higgins, an Australian scholar of secular Buddhism, so eloquently tells us, we can embrace the Buddha's teachings while abandoning the more supernatural and esoteric vestiges of ancestral Buddhism. This is easily accommodated because there is not one single, true, doctrinaire Buddhism which has survived millennia of oral traditions, varying cultural influences, and numerous interpreters. Nor is there one single, school of secular Buddhism.

Gotama delivered his teachings without presenting them as religious dogma or divine messages. He delivered practical knowledge to his followers about human suffering and its reduction. Secular Buddhists view Gotama as a human teacher who studied life deeply before sharing useful methods for living well. We do not worship him as a spiritual or divine figure.

According to a secular understanding of the dharma, suffering, also translated as dissatisfaction, is an inherent part of the human experience. It arises not from moral failure or divine punishment but from the way our minds process the world. As a psychologist, this concept is deeply resonant with my training and perspective. Our minds operate through three fundamental tendencies: craving what we don't have, clinging to what we do have, and resisting the inevitable changes of life. These tendencies are not flaws, but simply the way the human mind functions. By recognizing these patterns, we can learn to work with them more skillfully, reducing their hold on us, so alleviating unnecessary suffering.

The Buddha's teachings focus on present-moment awareness instead of leaving the world behind or seeking another existence. The teachings of the Buddha guide us to approach life with both curiosity and care while fully engaging with our present circumstances.

Batchelor presents Buddhism as a 'culture of awakening' which provides methods to develop mindfulness, emotional strength and ethical awareness when dealing with life's difficulties. The current world situation makes this approach highly suitable as we seek purpose and security during times of unpredictability.

Gotama's teachings are seen by secular Buddhists as experiments to be tested in real life. Having a practice that enables us to put these teachings to the test and determine their effectiveness. The Buddha's middle way concept serves as a practical solution for many aspects of contemporary life, showing that wellness emerges from balanced and attentive living rather than the extremes of either strict regulations or excessive behavior. The middle way teaches us to find equilibrium in all aspects of life through mindful moderation.

Gotama revealed that although suffering cannot be avoided, we all possess the ability to transform our experience of it. Secular Buddhism helps us deal with our suffering but it cannot guarantee complete elimination of pain or a flawless existence. The practice provides effective methods to handle challenging situations more effectively.

Mindfulness serves as an example of this practice. Through non-judgmental present-moment awareness, we start to detect small-scale reactions to experiences. The tendency to either resist what is aversive or try to hold onto impermanent things which are pleasurable only leads to increased suffering. This occurs as manifesting through past-focused rumination, future-oriented worry, or external blame. The practice of mindfulness helps us stop this pattern of behavior, enableing us to create mental space to help us handle life's problems with better clarity and composure.

Being trapped in traffic while going to a crucial appointment is a perfect example. The natural occurrence of frustration and anxiety intensifies when we actively resist the situation through mental battles. We ruminate on statements such as, 'this should not be happening' and 'I should have left earlier'. Practicing mindfulness does not eliminate traffic congestion, but it does enable us to choose not to fight the reality of the situation. Releasing our need for things to be different allows us to discover greater peace in challenging situations.

Rather than following strict religious rules, secular Buddhism asks us to tread an eightfold path – to follow ethical principles which function as life guidance for personal and social harmony. Ethics are presented through the lens of care instead of black-and-white rule-based systems.

The Buddha taught non-harming as a method to help us understand how our actions impact ourselves and others. The practice requires us to determine methods which protect others and bring positive results to ourselves. The flexible nature of this method enables us to handle life situations with integrity and compassion.

Moreover, secular Buddhism is not about becoming a Buddhist in any sense. The teachings of secular Buddhism remain accessible to anyone who wants to benefit from them. They do not require any rituals, belief in karma or rebirth, or membership in a Buddhist community. Rather, the practice involves adding basic yet meaningful techniques to our everyday lives.

Secular Buddhism stands out because it integrates well with contemporary neuroscience and psychology. Batchelor explains that the Buddha's teachings exist as active concepts which transform us according to the needs of different situations.

Most western sanghas, which are communities of those following the Buddha's teachings, are welcoming, inclusive, and equalitarian, unlike the hierarchical, monastic-led sanghas of ancestral schools of Buddhism.

Thich Nhat Hanh, the late Vietnamese monk, teaches us to find happiness now, and not to wait until our suffering reaches zero (which it will never do!) before we can experience joy. Human existence brings inevitable challenges and suffering. The presence of suffering does not require us to delay our pursuit of happiness.

The practice enables us to discover moments of joy, in spite of the challenges we face. We are encouraged to study human imperfections with kindness and understanding. Our ability to view suffering as an inherent part of life enables us to create space where happiness can exist alongside challenges.

The practice of secular Buddhism does not require that we gain a new religious identity or subscribe to specific beliefs. Secular Buddhists see it as a philosophy of living. It helps us understand how to live with mindful awareness, moral integrity, and compassionate care. The practice enables us to handle life's challenges with dignity and strength.

The journey on this path demands dedication and tolerance, along with a readiness to face reality. It demands courage, continuous work and tolerance, and a willingness to experience life exactly as it presents itself. The benefits, though, are many, and include more joy, stronger relationships, and a clearer life direction.

My intention

A word about my intention in writing this book. In my 35 years of studying and practicing the dharma, I found that many books and teachings on the topic were too general, abstract, esoteric, or non-specific to be readily applicable to the challenges of daily life. Adding the tools of modern, evidence-based psychology which align with the Buddha's teachings provides a more robust and practical dimension to the dharma. This has been key to my positive transformation, as well as that of my students.

Apply the concepts of practical dharma to your personal experiences. Observe which methods produce results. Life does not need to be flawless for you to experience contentment. Greater contentment exists right now in this imperfect world. I invite you to join me on the journey.

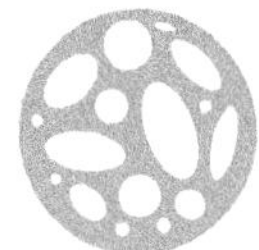

2. Understanding suffering

There are only two tragedies in this life; one is not getting what one wants, and the other is getting what one wants.

Oscar Wilde

Suffering when we do not get what we want is obvious. But what about suffering when we get what we want? The tragedy then is that it never lasts, so we suffer. This is the nature of impermanence that Gotama so brilliantly described.

One of the things that most appealed to me about Buddhism was the acknowledgment and normalizing of suffering in life, along with a means to address that suffering. The field of psychology does likewise. In other faith traditions, suffering, which is part of the human experience, is typically addressed by the promise of an afterlife that is suffering-free. In other words, suffering may be without relief in this life, but will be lifted in a promised next life.

Both large and small, suffering is everywhere in our lives and we, as humans, engage in various tactics and strategies to avoid it. Unfortunately, we cannot buy, achieve, accumulate, succeed, drink, drug, or have enough sex to totally overcome suffering. Try as we might to ignore it, avoid it, run from it, deny it, or cover it up with all kinds of activity, distractions, and mental gymnastics, at the end of the day we still suffer. Rarely do we have difficulty with pleasant things other than the fact they never last. We welcome the 10,000 joys of life for as long as they last, but do our best to avoid the 10,000 sorrows that the Taoists teach.

I view suffering as one of the most effective teachers on the spiritual path. It calls our attention to dysfunctional aspects of our life, so we can no longer ignore them. It is like a toothache that continues to hurt until we go to the dentist. It is a spiritual wake-up call. In my experience, many people have found their way to the dharma as a result of wanting to do something about their suffering.

I grew up in a family overflowing with dysfunction. Early in life I unconsciously concluded that the standard in my family was to be perfect in every way – grades, manners, and behavior. I would then be rewarded with the love and acceptance that all children need and crave. I was made to believe that being perfect was the way I needed to alleviate my suffering. Entering puberty, I realized that this strategy was not working. I went in the opposite direction, rebelling against everyone and everything. But that did not work either. My suffering got worse.

In early adulthood, it took the form of anxiety, depression, and dysfunctional relationships. I felt a painful separation from everyone and everything. I felt ashamed, as if I was the only one suffering from isolation, loneliness, and alienation. The faith tradition in which I was raised provided no relief, nor did it give me a perspective that enabled me to understand or make sense of the suffering in which I was immersed.

Overwhelmed by pain, I was highly motivated to find a way out of my suffering, something that psychotherapy was partially helpful in achieving. My introduction to the dharma completed the search. Once I began a regular meditation practice, and was studying the teachings, I knew I was on the right path toward finding some answers.

In the 35 years since I embraced the Buddhist path, every aspect of my life has been better in immeasurable ways. Once I understood and accepted my suffering, and leaned into it by embracing it head-on rather than running from it, light bulbs began to turn on.

Accepting that my suffering was the product of the causes and conditions that I grew up with was vital. I was not bad, nor did I need to feel ashamed of who I was. I was not weak for suffering. As much as I hated it, my suffering was a gift. It brought me to Buddhism, and the understanding and relief I sought.

The dharma suggests that we embrace our suffering with two outcomes in mind. The first is that by accepting and welcoming our suffering without judgment we reduce it. The second is to reduce the suffering of those with whom we are close, and who have been subjected to our unskillful and hurtful actions that were a product of acting-out or externalizing our suffering.

In the west, we tend to feel guilty and ashamed when we suffer, as if we are defective for not meeting the western ideal of perfection. This is not the Buddhist view. Gotama's teachings spoke to me as nothing else had – I knew immediately that I had found my spiritual path, and my spiritual home. Buddhism provided a framework and context in which my suffering finally made sense to me. It showed me the sources of my suffering and all the things I was habitually doing to perpetuate it. I no longer experienced it as a defect, a failing, something about which I should feel ashamed.

One of the many things that a dharma path has helped me see is that I am able to feel compassion for my suffering. Self-compassion is essential to healing, and requires that we acknowledge our suffering without shame. Shame about our suffering forces us to hide, deny, avoid, and disavow it. Compassion for ourselves is a powerful antidote to this shame. Our suffering can be a gift that teaches us and points us toward compassion for ourselves and others. My motivation to become a Buddhist teacher and introduce this path to others arose out of the powerful impact of the teachings in my own life.

I have deep gratitude for how this path has reduced my suffering. As I say to my students, 'if it can work for me, it can work for anyone' – provided there is a willingness to commit to the path, with regular meditation practice. Participation in a community, or sangha, is also critically important. With so many online offerings for community, this shouldn't be difficult.

Thich Nhat Hanh, the recently deceased Vietnamese monk, said, 'No mud, no lotus'. By this he meant that we try to avoid suffering, or cover it up, because it can feel so bad. Until we can face our suffering (the mud), we cannot be present and available to life, so that happiness and joy (the lotus) will continue to elude us. Without the mud for nourishment, the lotus cannot bloom.

Let's take a deeper look into suffering. Gotama stated – paradoxically – that accepting our suffering is a path to reducing our suffering. I noted earlier that suffering is too narrow a translation of the Pali word, dukkha. It also encompasses dissatisfaction, uneasiness, anxiety, annoyance, and worry. Let's agree that suffering is any state of unease that we experience.

Variations of this experience might include not getting what we crave, not getting enough of what we crave, not having our expectations for what we crave met, getting what we want but worrying about losing it, or getting what we crave and becoming bored with it. This list is not exhaustive but gives you a flavor of how varied the experience of suffering can be. The Buddha was even more nuanced in breaking down the experiences of suffering into three categories.

In the first category, the Buddha described the type of suffering that occurs with unpleasant physical or mental experiences.

Without fail, our lives will include unpleasant experiences, but routine unpleasant experiences are not what the Buddha meant by this first type of suffering. Our aversion to unpleasant experience is what constitutes this first category of suffering. The origin of this type of suffering is our craving or longing that the circumstances of our lives be different, that the unpleasantness cease.

The situations with which we are unhappy are typically not subject to change. This leaves changing our response to the unpleasant experience as our only option to reduce our suffering. If we can accept unpleasant feelings and sensations, be fully present with them, and recognize their impermanence, this type of suffering will be reduced. This was a brilliant insight that requires noticing, pausing, and discernment. For example, if I cut my finger it hurts. Physical pain is unavoidable but if I avoid engaging in the mental activity of craving that my cut finger should not hurt (that is, accept it), this type of suffering doesn't arise. The physical pain from my cut finger will run its course as it is impermanent. The mental anguish only occurred when I responded with aversion to the physical pain. That is, when I long for it to disappear and be replaced with pleasant or neutral sensations and feelings, an unrealistic craving.

The second category of suffering that the Buddha described occurs when we go beyond simple aversion in response to a negative physical or mental experience and add stressful thoughts about it. This includes judgments, rules, and anxious thoughts and questions. The Buddha brilliantly illustrated this teaching in the parable of the two arrows. He taught that the first arrow which strikes us represents an unavoidable source of suffering, like my cut finger. The second arrow is self-inflicted and is the suffering that we add to the original injury with our mental and emotional reaction to the pain from the first arrow. While the teaching focuses on the physical injury caused by the arrow, it applies to all the challenges we encounter.

When I could, with mindful awareness, accept the unpleasant nature of the pain of my cut finger, the first category of suffering did not arise. It arose only when I reacted with aversion by wishing for the pain to stop. The second category of suffering was not far behind in the form of second-arrow mental activity such as, 'How dumb of me that I cut my finger'. 'What if it gets infected?' 'I have too much to do. I don't have time for this'. The suffering here originated from the anxiety-filled stories I concoct about my injured finger.

Several years ago, one of my close friends died. The first type of suffering arose in me when I felt an aversion to my grief. I did not want to feel that pain, and when I added thoughts such as, 'I will be so lonely', 'this grief may make me ill', 'who will I do fun things with without my friend'. I was in the throes of the second category of suffering. The challenge is to bring these thoughts into conscious awareness, set them aside, and let them go. Acceptance creates an experience of spaciousness about an event enlarging our perspective. Engaging in the mental activity described changes nothing and only adds to suffering.

With mindfulness practice (within or outside of formal meditation) we become aware of whatever sensations or feelings are arising by noticing either outside stimuli (someone playing drums loudly next door), body stimuli (that painful cut finger), or from the thoughts that arise in response to these stimuli. If the stimulus is unpleasant, our mental reaction can range from a simple craving for it to stop (first category) to the mental formations of the second category, such as 'if he doesn't stop playing those drums, I'm going to flip out'.

As our practice deepens, we can shift our focus from the feeling tone of our experience to its impermanent nature. Seeing the impermanence of all phenomena shows us that trying to control an experience and make it pleasant only increases our suffering.

This is where we start letting go of wishing for life to be other than it is in the moment. Achieving this is what is often referred to as, 'holding it all'. We complement the process by watching our thinking without getting hooked by our thoughts or the stories we tell ourselves.

The third category of suffering that Gotama described also originates in craving. While the first two categories occur in response to unpleasant experiences, the third category arises in response to pleasant ones. When we enjoy a pleasant experience, we crave for it to continue and suffer when it does not. The craving is often present during the pleasant experience. We experience underlying displeasure when we are having a good time because it will not last.

My family goes to Jamaica in the winter. I might sit on the beach after dinner enjoying the natural beauty of the island and the breeze off the sea. This is something I look forward to all year. Yet I always have a nagging feeling that something is amiss. I realized over time, thanks to the practice of practical dharma, that I was experiencing the third category of suffering that the Buddha described.

The sunset I was observing would not last as my focus was on not wanting the sun to set rather than the moment's beauty. The Buddha taught that 'nothing that is impermanent can ever be satisfactory'. He understood that the transience of all worldly phenomena can negate pleasant experience.

Our experience of transience can only successfully be handled by coming to terms with the temporary nature of all things, noticing and accepting this fact. Simply put, by craving permanence we suffer because we will never get it. Again, we are reminded that grasping and craving underlie all types of suffering since we are wanting life to be other than it is.

So how do we manage the types of suffering? First, and very

importantly, we must become aware of when suffering is present. If we do not notice it, we are on autopilot, flying blind. This requires mindfulness and discernment because all three kinds of suffering are subtle and often hard to recognize. It requires the contact with the present moment that the dharma offers us.

When we feel dissatisfied, we have to stop and notice our suffering. From that point, we examine our experience with discernment until we find the place where we are not getting what we want, or are getting what we do not want. Then, we consciously try to let go of this craving and remind ourselves to accept the circumstances of life as they are at that moment.

As with the Jamaican sunset, I became aware that during a most pleasant experience I felt a bit of unease and dissatisfaction. I then examined that dissatisfaction until I found the source – my wish for that sunset to last forever. Of course, as Gotama fully understood, that could never happen.

By embracing the concept of impermanence, I could consciously choose to let go of my craving for the sunset to be other than a temporary phenomenon. Having done so I was free to enjoy, in that moment, the pleasant experience for as long as it lasted. Too often, however, we are so busy worrying about an enjoyable experience ending that we fail to enjoy it. To paraphrase a popular bumper sticker: 'suffering happens'.

Getting to the root of our suffering – this constant dissatisfaction in our lives – opens an opportunity to let go of grasping and craving. When we are not getting what we want, or getting what we do not want, we need to stop and consciously choose to let go of that craving. As we let go of the clinging, even for only a few seconds or minutes, we get a taste of freedom. Freedom has an expansive, open quality to it. At that moment, suffering ceases, as described in the third of the four tasks – that the end of suffering is possible through the abandonment of craving, we experience the freedom and peace that arises when craving subsides.

The eightfold path contains Gotama's complete treatment plan for understanding suffering by abandoning craving. It is the cure for the 'dis-ease' of suffering and provides the path that offers us the possibility of fulfilling our human potential through the cultivation of wisdom, ethical intentions, and mindfulness. All we need to do is avail ourselves of it.

Reflection

✦   We often think that if only we try hard enough or achieve enough success, we can eliminate suffering in our lives. How does it feel knowing that suffering is an inevitable and unavoidable part of life?

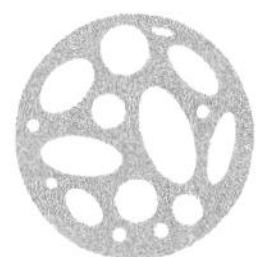

3. Impermanence and change

All conditioned things are impermanent – when one sees this with wisdom, one turns away from suffering.

The Buddha

Impermanence and acceptance are often taught together because they are so closely related. Without accepting that all phenomena are impermanent, inconstant, or unreliable we are not seeing the world as it is. We are stuck wishing it otherwise which is a sure path to suffering.

One of Gotama's many brilliant insights, impermanence is central to understanding why and how humans suffer. It is one of the three characteristics of existence that he taught, the other two being not-self and suffering.

For many, not-self is an elusive concept. A popular misconception is that we have no identity. Not-self refers instead to the absence of a fixed, unchanging self that is permanent. It is also the source of the ego we spend so much time and energy protecting and defending. Whenever we say, 'I am (fill in the blank)', we are identified with, and show our attachment to, the idea of a fixed self or ego.

Simply stated, impermanence means that everything is constantly changing including ourselves. Gotama said, 'all conditioned things are impermanent'. It is not impermanence per se that causes suffering; rather, it is our clinging to things to try and make them permanent. Acceptance of the universality of impermanence is central to the Buddhist path of reducing suffering. It is a key tenet of the path and underlies all the other teachings.

Acceptance as a practice is an antidote to avoidance of seeing life as it is, not as we want it to be. It is a practice that confronts our longing for persons, places, and things to be permanent.

For example, suppose I want my loved ones to live forever or, at the very least, outlive me. I cling to that wish and do not accept that I have no control over that outcome. My clinging creates suffering in the form of incessant worry about the well-being of my loved ones. I am so busy worrying that I miss the joy of spending time with them. Or, I want the shiny new smartphone which I craved to continue to bring me joy and happiness forever. When the novelty of the phone wears off, as it indeed will, I suffer due to the disappointment of it no longer making me happy and excited. An essential element of accepting impermanence is letting go of fixed ideas about how we want the world to be, despite having no control over it.

When I grew up in the 1950s, a boy would excitedly collect cereal box tops to send in for the free toy graphically displayed on the back of every box of Kellogg cereal. After several months, once I had the required number of box tops, I would mail them in with great anticipation. My longing for the toy to arrive was so great that I could feel it in my body. I suffered from the tension. Every day I would rush home from school and check the mail on the hall table to see if my toy had arrived. I thought about it constantly, and even though the excitement was positive, it was a form of suffering due to its all-consuming nature. Finally, after what seemed like months, I arrived home from school to see a package with a return address of Kellogg. Without fail, the toy was a cheap trinket, the novelty of which almost immediately dissipated. My suffering then took the form of deep disappointment both at the cheapness of the toy and because my weeks of suffering in the form of my longing had come to naught. Such is the nature of our suffering.

In its many forms, avoidance of reality keeps us from facing life as it is and from accepting the sorrows of this human life. Whenever we engage in wishful thinking about the status of people, places, or things, we invite suffering into our lives.

Humans suffer, and this can be debilitating. Our psychological pain includes difficult emotions and thoughts, unpleasant or painful memories, unwanted urges and sensations. We think about them, worry about them, resent them; we anticipate and dread them. We try to get rid of the pain which amplifies it, entangles us further in it, and potentially transforms it into something traumatic.

Humans resist the idea that life is filled with uncertainty. Simply put, we do not like it and try to deny it. Uncertainty about the future makes us anxious so we invent stories, beliefs, superstitions, and doctrines to try to reduce the uncertainty in our lives. We try to control the future, be it five minutes from now or five years from now. Without accepting that the future is unknowable, and that we have little to no control over it, we engage in fruitless worry and anticipation, and suffer accordingly. Letting go and accepting that we cannot know what lies ahead brings a great deal of freedom and reduced suffering in our day-to-day lives.

None of this is to say that we are not resilient or capable of coping with adversity when it does occur. Humans have the capacity for courage, compassion, and the ability to face tragic circumstances. Adversity and uncertainty do not stop us from loving, dealing with hurt and loss, and being present with all of life.

Avoidance of painful emotions and facts are primary sources of our suffering. What is it we do not accept? The list includes our bodies aging, loss of youthful vigor, conflicts with others, past failures or regrets, old resentments, financial stress, and unmet goals, to name a few.

As a practicing psychologist, I treated people with phobias and other anxiety disorders. From years of research, we know that avoidance of that which is frightening or painful is at the root of anxiety disorders, including phobias. When we avoid an anxiety-provoking situation by removing ourselves from it we strengthen the anxiety; we become more afraid, not less. While avoidance stops the anxiety in the moment, over time it makes the object of avoidance stronger and the anxiety greater. Our world shrinks as we engage in more and more avoidance of what frightens us. This is the psychological concept of experiential avoidance, which is avoiding not just that which is external but just as importantly that which is internal, including thoughts, feelings, and sensations that are painful, unpleasant, or frightening. Have we not all said in the face of something frightening or unpleasant, 'I don't want to think about that'.

In my field of psychology, there is the concept of creative hopelessness, the experience of seeing that our efforts to fix a problem are only making it worse. For example, recognizing the unworkability of experiential avoidance. It is waking up to the fruitlessness of our attempts to control our inner experiences. This opens the door for our willingness to make room for new possibilities such as accepting the situation as it is, not as we want it to be. We can then begin letting go of what is not working.

So, what exactly does it mean to let go? It is the opposite of clinging or grasping to persons, places, beliefs, experiences, or things. It is the acceptance of things as they are, not as we want them to be. For example, if I am stuck in traffic I can curse, fret, and become upset that the traffic is not moving when I have somewhere to be. Or, I can accept that there is absolutely nothing that I can do about the traffic jam. Instead, I focus on relaxing and accepting the situation by focusing on my breathing rather than generating mental messages that frustrate and aggravate me. In other words, I let go.

The most effective psychological treatment for anxiety disorders is facing our anxieties in what is known as graduated exposure to the anxiety-producing situation. This is 'psych-speak' for saying that we must face our fears or they will control us. The adage we use in therapy for anxiety disorders and other emotional suffering is, 'what we resist, persists'. This change requires a willingness and the courage to have our unpleasant experiences. The Buddha understood this over 2400 years ago. He said that transformation happens 'when suffering is known'. When we accept and face, or lean into, our suffering – anxiety, fear, and scary places – we can change our relationship to them and obtain freedom. I have seen this in my life and hundreds of times in my clinical work.

One of our biggest challenges is accepting the impermanence of our lives and those we love. The paradox of loss is that it opens our hearts and strips away our protective armor, whether we want it to or not. As we open to the experience of loss, accept it and lean into it rather than avoid it, we step more fully into the experience of loss. We feel a lightening of the load. In other words, we are more psychologically flexible. We are still sad and feel grief but are better able to ride the waves of our grief.

As our acceptance grows so does our experience of freedom; of being able to be with what is present in the moment despite the pain. Facing that which we want to turn away from with compassion and without judgment is truly a path to freedom. We shift from a judgmental and controlling stance about our internal experience to a compassionate and accepting perspective. We stop working so hard to repress or avoid that which is painful and understand that doing so only worsens our suffering.

Acceptance leads to freedom because it makes us more psychologically resilient and more able to embrace all experiences.

Emotional rigidity and inflexibility, including fixed ideas about how life should be and strict adherence to rules, are the cause of much suffering. With acceptance, we do not waste energy avoiding things. We are not shut down and emotionally contracted or constantly in avoidance mode. Rather, we are open to whatever life hands us which results in true freedom. The opposite of not opening to all experience is to constrict, avoid, and deny. With acceptance, we move from resistance to embracing life as it is.

I would like to share an experience of true acceptance of impermanence that I witnessed several years ago. One of my best friends was someone I met over four decades ago. We remained close friends up until his death a few years ago. Though we lived in different states my family vacationed with him and his family every summer. Our children grew up together. My friend was very successful in business and lived as full a life as anyone you will ever meet. He traveled the world and climbed mountains; he lived life with energy, passion, and presence.

In 2010, after several years of undiagnosed problems, he was diagnosed with a rare form of cancer for which there was no specific treatment protocol. My friend immediately began an aggressive treatment regimen as he was unwilling to accept that his life would end so early. He fought the disease with every means he could muster. My wife and I begin traveling every three to four weeks to spend time with him and his family and to offer presence and support. I spent hours talking to him about his life and his difficulty accepting his imminent death.

I was fortunate to watch his transformation from fighting the inevitable to accepting the reality of his death. It was a profound teaching on letting go and accepting the impermanence of our existence. He relaxed and his sense of humor returned. He could appreciate the gift that his life had been, including the people he loved and who loved him. The last time I saw him before he died, he was a shadow of his former self. I held him, and told him I loved him. He was semi-conscious but I knew he had heard me. His wife later told us that he died peacefully after we returned home, surrounded by her and their children.

My friend's acceptance of the inevitability of his death brought him a sense of peace at the end that was profound to witness. He showed the true meaning of acceptance during one of the most challenging times in our lives. Though my loss was profound I am grateful for the teaching that he provided me.

Reflection

✦ Acknowledging the reality of impermanence can be unsettling as we feel out of control. What is your reaction to the teaching on impermanence?

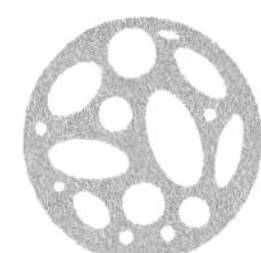

4. Ego and self-identity

It's in the act of having to do things that you don't want to that you learn something about moving past the self. Past the ego.
bell hooks

Did you know that the Buddha never instructed us to rid ourselves of a separate self or ego? Or that we should hide behind it, or drape it in spiritual language to avoid dealing with our emotional baggage. Our challenge is to develop a healthy sense of self/ego that recognizes its ever-changing quality and frees us from fixed ideas about who or what we are, particularly when those fixed ideas reflect a tendency toward self-aggrandizement or grandiosity.

My decision to include a separate chapter on the self/ego reflects my bias as a clinical psychologist. I am not referring to ego in the sense that Freud talked about it – as part of the triad of id, ego and super-ego, which has specific theoretical implications. I am using the term to refer to our sense of a separate self; the fragile thing we work so hard to inflate, protect, defend and hold up. While the Buddha never used the term ego, we have adopted it to connote the sense of self he described. As much as we try to believe otherwise, our sense of self – of who we are – is neither fixed nor permanent. Our experience is ever-changing.

Over the many years of my professional career, I saw in my office the suffering caused by the ego daily. Much human suffering is a function of protecting the ego from shame and invalidation, and the seeking of ways to obtain admiration and aggrandizement. The teachings of the Buddha comprised part of the toolkit that I used to address the suffering of my psychotherapy patients that was caused by the ego.

Ego is a mental construct that consists of the lifetime of stories we tell ourselves, representing the totality of our life experiences filtered through an emotional lens. The filter with which we see and experience the world combines our genetics, brain chemistry, home life as children, conditioning, peer relationships, economic circumstances, and other experiences that we accumulate over a lifetime. The ego internalizes all the successes and failures of our life, including all the joys and sorrows. It is our conscious self, how we interact with the world around us. It is who we tell ourselves we are and is often distorted out of self-interest.

The ego is never static or fixed. It can be either inflated, as seen with narcissism, deflated as seen with low self-esteem and depressive disorders, or it can be balanced with a realistic sense of our strengths and weaknesses. It changes from moment to moment, depending on external and internal circumstances.

The ego seeks happiness, gratification, recognition, and the fulfillment of sensual desire. Everything that we identify with is part of our ego, the conscious experience of who we are from which we unconsciously try to edit and exclude the negative qualities.

The ego is where the shame-pride continuum exists, a well-accepted concept in clinical psychology. Simply stated, when we feel adequate within ourselves, the ego feels pride. When we feel inadequate, the ego feels shame. Shame and pride exist at opposite ends of a continuum; we vacillate continually along this continuum. We feel inflated when we are filled with pride and deflated when we are filled with shame. We try to meet the world with a pride-filled ego, since doing so reveals what we consider to be our most attractive traits. We try to keep shameful parts hidden from both ourselves and others out of fear of being judged or rejected.

This trait of humankind, this ego, has caused untold suffering in the world over the millennia. It is all about I, me, and mine. Ego is where emotional reactivity originates. It is where greed, hatred, and delusion – the three poisons – manifest. The source of comparing ourselves with others and external standards is the ego.

But the ego is not something to get rid of, even if we could. We need a healthy ego to function. We also need to see where it causes great suffering and alienation from others. Monitoring the ego with mindful noticing, pausing, and discerning, we learn where the expression of ego needs is unskillful and causes suffering and harm. We have agency to manage our unwholesome ego needs only if we are aware of them.

A healthy sense of self lives in the present moment as much as possible, having relinquished fixed ideas about itself, either laudatory or negative. It guides us toward seeing our interconnectedness to all things as part of a much larger context. A healthy sense of self becomes less about our selfish motives and more about the greater good.

We could not function in the world without a sense of self. It is the mental template that guides us every minute of every day. We need to have preferences and make choices. Our impulse control, based in our sense of self, puts the brakes on our worst tendencies in what is known as executive function. We seek to cultivate a healthy and honest understanding of who we are, warts and all; we do not deny the problematic attitudes and behaviors. Instead, we work to recognize and accept them – which we can only do when we honestly embrace and admit them. We cease seeking happiness outside of ourselves and stop trying to make ourselves special in the world. No longer do we use avoidant, compulsive, or distracting behaviors to deny who we are.

It took me years of dharma practice and study to truly understand this path and set a skillful means of walking it. While I still have a way to go, my awareness of where I need to go and where I trip up is more evident. It has been and continues to be painful to admit to and acknowledge my shadow side. By incorporating self-compassion and self-forgiveness in the exploration, I can address my shadow with less shame and self-recrimination. I began to see that the worse I felt about myself, the harder I tried to look good and inflate myself with others, which only served to alienate them. Such is the imbalance caused by trying to fix a negative self-assessment.

Our work with the ego is not that of renunciation of all earthly pleasures, self-denial, or asceticism. It does not mean denying the joy in our lives, or not having fun. It is an honest and balanced reassessment of who and what we are, shorn of all the baggage we pile on to look good, reassure ourselves, deny our negative qualities, and support our self-delusions.

As my practice deepened over the years, it became more apparent that much of the narrative I had developed about myself was a fiction to cover and soothe wounds from my early life. Yet I worried that I would collapse into nothingness if I gave up that story. The narrative is what we psychologists call the 'false self,' a concept developed by the British psychiatrist D.W. Winnicott in the 1950s. The false self is the persona or mask we put on like armor early in our lives to try and overcome early trauma and defend ourselves in the world.

Psychologists distinguish between highly traumatic events like abuse and neglect and so-called 'everyday trauma' to connote the normal, but painful, slings and arrows of the human developmental experience. But even everyday trauma is painful, and we work hard to protect ourselves from experiencing it.

My false self has many facets, as they do. One of the more prominent ones growing up was that of the 'good boy'. Outward appearances reigned supreme in my southern American, privileged, white, upper-middle-class family. No one asked, knew, or wanted to know, what my internal experience was as long I looked good on the outside for the world to see. The standard was perfect manners, grooming, behavior, and performance – at school and elsewhere. All my basic survival needs for shelter, food, clothing, and material comfort were met by my parents. I wanted nothing regarding such needs. Yet, I was very lonely, as the experience was of never being seen or understood for who I indeed was – that real person beneath all the outward appearances.

This was a source of great suffering throughout my early life and young adulthood. I did not understand why I was unhappy. I was following all the rules and striving to be the good boy. Had I been sold a bill of goods? Was it a massive fraud? I felt dead inside.

I knew no other way and no source of relief until a course of intensive psychotherapy in my 30s was followed by discovering the Buddhist path in my early 40s. When I began to delve into Buddhist teachings, I felt I finally had a way of understanding and confronting my suffering beyond what even therapy had provided. For more than thirty-five years that promise has held, though the work continues. The transformation in me has been profound regarding my self-acceptance and happiness, and the happiness of those I love.

I don't want to leave you with the impression that any of this is easy. Typically, we have to be in such a state of suffering that we are highly motivated to do what we need to do to start changing. It takes tremendous courage and tenacity to look honestly at our flaws and imperfections. We need a lot of self-compassion and self-forgiveness to navigate such tricky waters. A community of fellow travelers, such as a sangha or a 12-step group, can be invaluable on this journey.

As it evolved, western Buddhism incorporated the therapeutic culture of the west. This has largely been a positive trend. The addition of modern western psychological theory fits well with Buddhist teachings. The result is a much more robust means of reducing or attenuating suffering. The ego and the work required to manage it sit at the center of the combination of the two approaches.

Reflection

◆ How do you expend time and energy in the care and feeding of your ego? As you think about doing less so, what thoughts arise?

II • LET REACTIVITY BE

In this section, we review the sources of much, if not most, of our suffering; we see that instead of suppressing or denying these emotional challenges, we acknowledge and accept them as part of the human experience

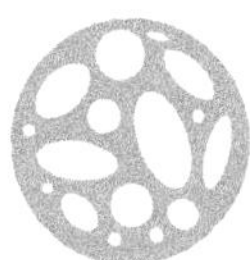

5. Reactivity and shame

Suffering can thus be seen in large part as a kind of resistance or reactivity to the pain of the present moment.

Donald Rothberg

Have you ever thought about the evolutionary purpose of shame? As with many other innate responses shame is a vestige of our evolutionary past. It is an emotion that became hardwired into our species as it evolved so our ancient ancestors were inhibited from exhibiting behaviors which would result in being banished from their family, community, or tribe. Evolution naturally selected those with a higher tendency for shame because banishment from the tribes of our ancestors 200,000 years ago on the savannahs of Africa meant certain death from starvation, predators, or hostile tribes. Those with a low capacity for shame were banished and did not survive when they behaved badly. They therefore did not pass their genes on to future generations.

Humans evolved to be shame-prone; it is considered a hard-wired emotion. In our lives, without mindful management, excessive or toxic shame is one of the primary causes of emotional reactivity and the resulting suffering. A primary challenge in practicing secular dharma is managing our emotional reactivity. Simply put, emotional reactivity is the problematic tendency to be controlled by our emotions.

Suffering almost always involves a degree of impulsive reactivity. Individuals living in a constant state of emotional reactivity are characterized as emotionally dysregulated, making stable relationships difficult and causing much suffering.

One of the basic tenets of Buddhist teaching is the need to learn to manage our emotions. The fundamental challenge in reducing reactivity and achieving equanimity is acceptance of things as they are, not as we want them to be. Suffice it to say our mind is not at ease, nor are we at peace, when we are in a state of emotional reactivity.

We exhibit psychological flexibility when our unskillful emotions are not battering us. Instead, we cope with, accept, and adapt to difficult situations. Such flexibility requires self-awareness through mindful discernment and contact with our core values.

Emotional reactivity has multiple triggers and manifestations – individual (shame and guilt), relational (anger and conflict), and social (taking sides). A popular term for emotional reactivity is 'hair trigger'.

Reactivity involves our conscious mind so we can, with practice, make choices about our reactivity so that we are not prisoners of, and governed by, our emotions. Decisions based on emotions rarely turn out well. We all have multiple triggers for our reactivity, the specific nature of which results from individual life experience.

In addressing reactivity, we first cultivate awareness by noticing and pausing. Then we can see with intention and discernment the pattern of our reactivity and how we become contracted in heart and mind. Each of us has unique recurring and predictable reactivity patterns based on our personal history.

Absence of reactivity is characterized by a sense of spaciousness and qualities of clarity, equanimity, and humility. We are calm, reflective, and experience equanimity. Our emotional stance is largely in balance. We are psychologically flexible in our dealings with the world and 'look before we leap' in most situations.

Experiences of greed, hatred/aversion, and delusion – the three poisons – are significant contributors to our reactivity. Emotional reactivity is often characterized as bondage; its absence is characterized by freedom from suffering.

Shame is a primary human emotion and central to our understanding of reactivity. Psychologists' study and understanding of shame exploded 40 years ago, forever changing the field. Because it is so important, we will examine it in more detail beginning with some definitions.

Guilt and shame are often confused though they frequently co-occur. Guilt is the result of a transgression against someone or something which typically focuses on external behavior. For example, if I break your lamp, I feel guilty. Guilt offers redemption and reconciliation through corrective words or actions. If I replace your lamp my guilt is reduced or eliminated. If I disparage you but then apologize my guilt is lessened.

Shame is different. We feel shame when we violate an internal or external standard to which we unconsciously subscribe. The focus is on our sense of self, our ego, and self-worth. With unhealthy toxic shame, we feel flawed, unlovable, and defective. For example, if I do not live up to perfectionistic standards in some aspect of my life I must be flawed or damaged. This is negative or toxic shame.

Healthy shame is an inborn emotion that helps govern our socially appropriate behavior. It is as necessary for our continued acceptance in our social group as it was true for our ancient ancestors. Embarrassment and feeling self-conscious are mild forms of shame, while humiliation is an intense form.

Positive morality is a result of healthy shame. In anticipation of feeling shame, I will avoid engaging in immoral, illegal, or socially unacceptable behavior, such as taking all my clothes off in public or eating with my hands in a fancy restaurant. Healthy shame signals us to put the brakes on our unskillful impulses to inhibit our most offensive tendencies and prevent negative judgment or rejection by others.

Shame becomes a problem and triggers reactivity when we attack ourselves for not meeting an arbitrary standard. If the experience is sufficiently intense, suicide can be the response in highly shame-prone cultures.

Violence will likely ensue if we feel shamed or disrespected by others. For example, road rage incidents typically have shame as the source of violent or reckless behavior. The emotional response is shame if one feels small, diminished, or disrespected, such as when cut off in traffic. The angry reactivity, born of shame, is then directed outwardly toward the other driver.

In Buddhism, healthy shame is the guardian of ethical and moral behavior. In his more general teachings, Gotama called shame-like emotions a 'bright guardian of the world' in that it kept people from betraying the trust of others. He also called shame-like emotions a 'noble treasure' which is more valuable than gold or silver because it protects us from doing things we would later regret.

The suffering from toxic shame, and the triggered reactivity, come from our often-unconscious clinging to the idea that we must live up to an unrealistic, if not perfectionist, standard in all aspects of our life. Another trigger is the belief that others should recognize our importance and treat us with proper deference. We work hard to protect the false self we created and not have it exposed lest we feel shame.

Connecting meaningfully with others when we are gripped by toxic shame is not possible. We are voiceless and want to withdraw, hide, and not be seen. Neither do we wish to be exposed and humiliated for the imagined defects and flaws that seem apparent to us. We do what we can to avoid feeling small and defective, often by wielding negative power over others, including abusive/aggressive behavior, or trying to inflate our external image with self-aggrandizement or the trappings of success. Again, the ego comes into play as it is our fragile sense of self that suffers shame.

In my work with shame, I discovered how feeling shame quickly triggered me to become reactive. A sign of my vulnerability to shame is feeling self-conscious around others: a red flag. When I felt self-conscious, I would vigilantly monitor my words and actions so as not to violate my internalized standard regarding appearances, a vestige of my family's expectations.

When triggered in my youth I came to an emotional fork in the road regarding shame. One fork was an attack on myself in which my sense of self collapsed. I wanted to tuck my tail between my legs and slink away, filled with self-loathing. The other fork, which became my default, was to feel rage toward whomever, or whatever, triggered me and from whom I felt judged or criticized. The bar for that feeling was low because my constructed false self was on a shaky foundation. Alternately, my rage was empowering unlike collapsing into self-loathing on the other fork. Other than feeling energized and self-protective, the rage fork was no less dysfunctional as it alienated others; I was again alone. I was filled with remorse for my behavior, triggering yet more shame. I could not find a way out of this dynamic and the pattern persisted.

As my Buddhist practice developed, I began to see options by employing our good friends: noticing, pausing, and discernment. Once I could see the pattern, I could bring practical dharma tools to bear on the problem. The cues to noticing were the feelings of rage that would start to arise in my mid-section when I felt ridiculed, criticized, exposed and shamed. I learned to pause and name it:

'I am having a shame attack'. Only then did I have the option to respond more skillfully and inhibit my reactivity, letting go of the urge to react.

Invoking self-compassion helps immensely as does the recognition that 'it's like this now'. In other words, the situation in which I find myself is what it is, not what I wish it were. I can either accept it or fight with it and keep my reactivity and suffering going.

When I am reactive it helps to reach out to a trusted other for connection – to be open about my pattern of reactivity and to gain perspective. While I still get triggered – usually when I am tired, hungry, or stressed – it happens less often and less intensely.

What are some specific examples of reactivity? They include flying off the handle, lashing out at others, angry withdrawal, speaking harshly to others, using self-protective mechanisms that further isolate us, self-judgment, and self-harm to name a few. If we dive deeper into reactivity, we see that it is often a function of the forces of craving and clinging to an idea that things, or we, should be different than they are – the foundation of all suffering.

Often shame is about an old emotional wound being reopened related to belonging, being seen, intimacy, or security. When we discover such wounds, we must respond to them with compassion toward ourselves and without judgment. Sharing our suffering with trusted others and receiving their compassion is also a powerful antidote. Meditation practice is a refuge that offers us the quiet contemplation to recognize these wounds. All our early life experiences, especially with our caregivers and attachment figures, shape our patterns of reactivity.

As a little boy, I was ridiculed for crying when I hurt myself. I developed a heightened awareness about being seen as sensitive which was viewed as a weakness for a boy in the 1950s. If someone suggested that I was overly sensitive, I lashed out defensively in the reactive way described. This has been one of the biggest challenges on my path. Growing up there was much scrutiny and ridicule in my family due to the emphasis on outward appearances.

I grew up feeling very defensive and hypervigilant, often perceiving ridicule by others where it did not exist. It was exhausting as I was always on guard and had no idea how else to be. I would get defensive, annoyed and angry, and withdraw if I perceived ridicule or even good-hearted teasing. It felt as though others did not care about me or know me. As a child, I never developed the ability to laugh at myself much less have others laugh at me. The experience reinforced my painful feelings of separateness from others, especially my siblings with whom I often felt at war. I reacted immediately without thinking, understanding, or processing my emotions. It was a vicious, self-defeating cycle.

The teachings of the dharma have helped me understand this process and given me the tools to work with it. The process begins with pausing, noticing the effects of perceived slights on my subjective world.

My first challenge was to set an intention to notice my reactivity once I had insight into what was happening. I had to learn to distinguish between responding versus reacting, which involved pausing, breathing into my body's tightness, letting go to release the pressure, and finally acting with intention and integrity.

Reactivity has physical correlates in the body manifesting as the release of stress hormones like adrenalin and cortisol, shallow breathing, muscle tension, and tunnel vision; it activates the sympathetic branch of the central nervous system known as fight, flight, or freeze. When this occurs our problem-solving and ability to interact constructively with others goes offline. Self-soothing and calming, taking a time out, breathing slowly for several breaths, and allowing the physiological responses to subside are all antidotes for the physical aspects of reactivity.

My ongoing challenge became meeting such reactive feelings with openness and compassion. Our path is always those aspects of life that most challenge us. Like the toothache that cannot be ignored, these triggers make us notice where we need to put our energy and effort to change. With practice, we move beyond reactivity to accepting our painful experiences and feelings without shame. Challenging emotions that are fully felt and mindfully held can be surmounted through wisdom and released – all the while remembering that the ground of the spiritual path we walk is the true nature of reality.

We learn to live our lives from an awakened heart and mind. A vital component of this journey is self-compassion which gives us the freedom, safety, and resolve to shine a light into the dark, ugly corners of our shadow selves. We move from reactivity to acceptance of all facets of who we are and all that we experience. Greater emotional regulation, psychological flexibility, and freedom follow.

I consider reactivity one of our biggest challenges as human beings given that we are nothing if not emotional creatures. Our emotions enrich our lives but they also can imprison us and take away our capacity for wise decisions and wise action.

Reflection

✦   Which emotions are most challenging for you in managing your reactivity more skillfully? Which tools to better manage your reactivity resonate with you?

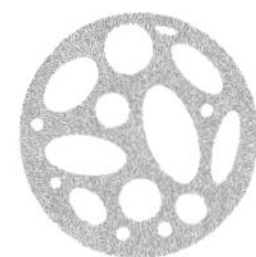

6. Desire and craving

Desires are not killed by fulfilling them.

Hermann Hesse

Given its prominence in our daily lives and the role of desire in our suffering, I want to dig deeper into desire. As I noted, all of the five hindrances disrupt our practice and impede our progress on the spiritual path. Any of the hindrances – sensual desire, ill-will, doubt, sloth and torpor, and restlessness/worry take us out of the present moment and alienate us from ourselves and others.

Desire is not a bad thing. We depend on our desires to survive: the desire for nourishment, hydration, warmth, shelter, and sex for procreation. The challenge we face is to distinguish between healthy and unhealthy desires. Poorly managed or uncontrolled desires quickly become compulsions or addictions – what Gotama called 'thirsts'. Unmanaged desires create tension that accompanies the craving. We are constantly distracted and think of little else but the source of our craving, as I was with my Kellogg toy. We live only on the surface of our lives as everything else becomes secondary to our preoccupation with our unskillful desires.

Sensual desire is fundamental as it involves 'feeding' our

senses of sight, smell, sound, taste and touch, our windows to the world. The Buddha included a sixth sense – that of thinking. However, when the pull of indulging any of the senses becomes too strong, we focus solely on satisfying the sense pleasure, accompanying it with the narrative that we create to justify it.

The stories we create about a sense desire become repetitive and powerful, especially when we are deprived of the opportunity to indulge the craving. Desire, a close cousin to craving and greed, is a compelling part of the human experience. During both meditation and daily life, we strive to watch our desires arise and pass away, as do all impermanent phenomena, rather than getting hooked into the story and gratification of the desire. Once a narrative hooks us we are on shaky ground. The further we are along the path of indulging unskillful choices the more difficult it is to recover, or pull back, with skillful means. I saw this phenomenon frequently in my psychology practice with patients.

Let me reiterate that there is nothing inherently wrong with sensual pleasure; it is a hindrance only when it interferes with our ability to stay present and be skillful in our choices. We depend on our desires to stay alive. By training ourselves to watch our desires arise we learn to discern between those which are healthy, those which are problematic, and those which cause suffering.

As we notice a strong desire arise, we pause. We ask ourselves: How strong is it? Where in the body is it showing up? What are the physical sensations accompanying it? What might underlie it – loneliness, sadness, self-criticism, and/or shame?

In my practice as a psychologist, I found with my patients that the desire and craving for sense pleasure could be a way of attempting to self-regulate painful or difficult emotions. Indulging in sensual desire is a form of experiential avoidance. We might include compulsive eating when not hungry, compulsive sex, intoxication with drugs or alcohol, compulsive spending, addictive gambling, spending hours on the internet, obsessive exercise, or anything else done to excess. Engaging in any of these compulsive behaviors distracts us from a painful inner life.

When we become familiar with the tendency toward compulsive sensual desire, freedom requires looking at the desire directly, naming it, and feeling how it is experienced in the body. Only then can we successfully begin to set it aside. By learning to experience it without judgment, the underlying painful emotion loses its grip on us.

When I compulsively eat chocolate, I am not addressing my poor mood. Instead, I am trying to distract myself. I pay the price by feeling bloated, putting on extra pounds, and causing a sugar rush followed by a crash. When I refrain from reaching for chocolate and instead bring mindful awareness to my unpleasant feeling state, I opt for the skillful route. The compulsion lessens when I resist and touch into the present-moment awareness of what I am feeling. As I become freer of the compulsive desire for sensual pleasure, my confidence grows, and the more likely I can decide wisely which desires or aspirations will govern my life. Not that I have completely given up my craving for chocolate. I do, however, indulge more mindfully and skillfully. If you have never eaten a chocolate bar mindfully, I highly recommend the practice. Just do it slowly and mindfully.

When we approach our desires with mindful awareness the habit of staying present becomes stronger over time and allows us to make better choices. We must also be mindfully aware of our physical and emotional state when confronted with a potent desire. For that reason, as an example, I suggest avoiding meditation on an empty stomach or when exhausted. The desire to eat or to nap will prove too great a distraction from present-moment awareness. It is not skillful to ignore awareness of our environment, both internal and external, when we are dealing with desire. We use discernment to assure that we do not set ourselves up for failure when managing our desires.

Discernment is critical to skillfully managing our desires. Do we see the desire accurately or just on the surface? Where is the desire coming up in the body? Are we able, with discernment, to see what is underneath it – a lack of connection to others, loneliness, sadness, irritation, shame, or other difficult emotional states?

As noted, addiction results from experiential avoidance of uncomfortable and unwanted thoughts or feelings. Having too many drinks at a party to ease social anxiety, using opiates to ease the pain of failure or trauma, or stimulants such as cocaine to avoid boredom or loneliness, are all forms of experiential avoidance.

Next, we turn our attention to exploring the subjective experience of strong desire rather than focusing only on the object of our desire. How strong is the inner pull to act on the desire? Where do I feel it in my body? Can I stay with the exploration rather than push it away with aversion, or indulging it? Again, we implement the tools of noticing, pausing, and discernment.

Desires are addressed skillfully by accepting them in full relief and not avoiding or denying them. Denied or disavowed unskillful desires can wreak havoc on our spiritual progress. This is why mindful self-awareness is such a critical practice. Our challenge is to accept without judgment, rather than to deny or eschew, the parts of ourselves we deem shameful or unattractive including our unskillful desires.

Forgoing the gratification of problematic desires requires self-awareness and the practices of restraint and renunciation, which are not easy tasks. When treating patients who were struggling with compulsions or addictions, the challenge was helping them look beyond the outward behavior, such as compulsive eating, to the underlying feeling states they were feeding. Once they could identify and name, without shame, the deep-seated feelings, such as inadequacy or defectiveness, we were on fertile ground. Focusing solely on external behavior was a dead end.

Our unskillful desires are often beyond our awareness because we are too close to them; they are the water we swim in. Practical dharma helps us pull back the cover so we can address them skillfully. When I was mindlessly stuffing chocolate in my mouth on autopilot, I had no clue what was driving my behavior. I only knew that I later regretted having eaten too much chocolate given the costs associated with doing so. The painful emotions I was trying to feed persisted. Using the tools available, the opportunity for change became real.

Reflection

✦ Over which of your desires do you feel that you have the least control? Which of the tools described can you enlist to help better manage your unskillful desires?

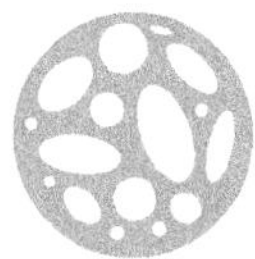

7. Anger and ill will

Anger leads to hate. Hate leads to suffering. When we hold onto feelings of anger, we do more damage to ourselves than the person we feel anger towards. The truth is, anger is a punishment we give ourselves for someone else's mistake.

Master Yoda from Star Wars

Have you ever tried to meditate or be fully present when angry? The urge to indulge ill will and anger is very powerful. We ruminate about it, dwell on our perceived wounds, replay the triggering event over and over in our minds, and plan revenge or retaliation. Our intention is to avenge the wound of our hurt pride, shame, and humiliation. We seek to even the score. We briefly looked at anger in the chapter on emotional reactivity. Ill will or anger is another one of the five hindrances and, as with sensual desire, is highly disruptive of our equanimity and serenity.

Revenge born of anger is a powerful impulse. Think about warfare over the course of history. One country attacks the other side. That side then attacks the opposing side in retaliation. On and on it goes with no end or solution in sight. Sadly, humankind has been reenacting this pattern since we stood upright if not before.

Our primate cousins, chimpanzees, engage in a similar pattern. Our capacity for ill will and violence is endless as are the triggers for it in our world.

When we are in the grip of anger it is impossible to be calm, reflective, and settled. We are not free but are prisoners of the hostile emotions which obscure our ability to see clearly and act skillfully. Rather, we are operating from emotional rigidity and our efforts to control situations and others; we lack emotional flexibility that helps us 'roll with the punches' with equanimity.

Ill will or anger result in emotional reactivity and are its primary causes. It manifests as resentment, annoyance, hostility, irritation, and potentially violence – all forms of emotional reactivity. People are killed because of ill will. Young men fueled by high testosterone levels, inflated pride, and the need to save face with their peers may choose death rather than appear weak or cowardly. When the easy availability of firearms is added to the mix, we have an epidemic.

The emotional reactivity born of anger and ill will takes many problematic forms including flying off the handle, lashing out, angry withdrawal, speaking harshly to others, using self-protective mechanisms that further isolate us, self-judgment, and self-harm to name a few. If we dive deeper into reactivity, we see that ill will is often a function of the forces of craving, as well as clinging to an idea that things should be different than they are – the foundation of all suffering.

When we are in a state of angry ill will, we want to hurt, punish, attack, push away, turn away, or withdraw from the person or situation that triggered us. Ill will manifests on a continuum from mild irritation and resentment to extreme violence.

We suffer when we are in a state of anger or ill will. It is painful and we contract physically and emotionally. We do not see the world clearly as our perceptions are skewed toward the negative.

We operate with a reactive hair trigger devoid of the noticing, pausing, and discerning that guide us toward a more skillful response.

Ill will is a great disrupter of relationships and our connections to others. We lash out, we blame, and we engage in alienating behavior. When we are in the grip of ill will we cannot interact well with others, and others avoid us so as not to be subjected to our hostility or other unskillful emotions. Ill will can be the product of underlying feelings of being defective or unlovable; so we preemptively strike out to avoid criticism and protect our ego, following the adage that the best defense is a good offense. We justify our anger by identifying with the role of a victim of the world's perceived unfair treatment of us. Ill will alienates others and we end up emotionally alone and isolated.

Before I embraced the dharma, people saw me as an angry person. They were correct as my temper was always lurking just below the surface of my emotions, waiting with hypervigilance to come out if I felt misunderstood, mocked, mistreated, or short-changed. Those close to me walked on eggshells so as not to trigger an outburst. They suffered from my outbursts and I suffered from the shame and isolation that resulted from my tantrums. This pattern was a primary source of suffering for all involved. I am very grateful that this pattern is no longer present thanks to my dharma practice.

Ill will is about the ego. Is the ego threatened? Ashamed? Embarrassed? Feeling unseen or unheard? Disregarded? Is our fragile sense of pride hurt? Are we interpersonally triggered, either real or vicariously? Am I being judgmental and annoyed because I am clinging to a fixed idea about how others should treat me? Have others disappointed me in some way? The triggers for our ill will are everywhere in our lives.

The prescription is familiar: we start with mindful noticing, pausing, and discernment. The pause is critical as it lets our nervous system relax, giving us the option of continuing to calm ourselves and generating a more skillful response. We offer compassion to ourselves and the source of our ill will and try to imagine the suffering of the other person that resulted in their problem behavior by which we felt triggered. We do not establish preconditions for those to whom we direct our compassion and those whom we exclude.

We do not judge our ill will as a personal failing. Rather we confront the self-serving view that the world is unfair, replacing it with a more spacious view that situations randomly happen to all of us. We let go of any sense of victimhood and understand that adversity is a normal part of the human journey, which we address skillfully with our mindfulness practice and the insights it produces.

Modern life provides us with an endless supply of things about which to feel ill will and anger. We are not captive to our more reptilian or lower brain functions. If given time to come online we have a cerebral cortex that will help us respond more skillfully. First, we have to notice and then build in a pause since the lower brain functions are immediate whereas the higher brain functions take longer to activate. Our challenge is to employ the lessons of the dharma and set an intention to act with wisdom and compassion when ill will or anger arises.

There are instances where collective ill will may create the illusion of connection with others who share our hostile outlook. Connection predicated on shared anger or hatred is neither real connection nor is it satisfying. It is not skillful, and is dangerous and divisive; it causes separation between people and groups. Sadly, this phenomenon is rampant in modern society.

One of the most effective antidotes to anger is the practice of forgiveness. Forgiveness is primarily for our benefit rather than for the person we are forgiving. When we forgive, we set down the weight of the ill will which causes us much suffering. We decide not to retaliate against the person who we feel harmed us. That person need not even know that we have forgiven them. To be clear – forgiving someone does not mean that we 'let them off the hook'. Rather, we eliminate their power over us which existed when we are consumed by ill will toward them.

Ill will/anger and their close cousin reactivity cause us individually, those around us, and society, tremendous suffering. We must bring all the tools of our spiritual path to bear on the challenges they present.

Reflection

✦ How do you typically handle anger? What is the role of your ego in anger or ill will?

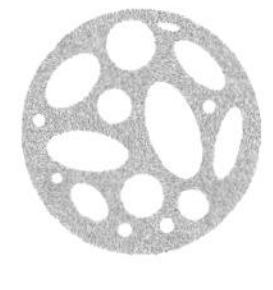

8. Anxiety

Humans hate uncertainty. We want control and predictability and to know the future. Uncertainty, a lack of control, and unpredictability make us anxious.

Human survival needs drive these tendencies, as was particularly true for our ancient ancestors who needed to anticipate and plan, particularly regarding food supply and safety. Planning anxiety goes beyond basic survival needs into nonspecific fears for our survival. This was particularly true in an ancient world where random events could pose a threat.

Humans, because of our capacity for language and imagination, experience fear and anxiety regularly. Because we have a thinking brain, we experience fear and anxiety in ways that creatures without a cerebral cortex do not. This experience is part of our evolutionary heritage. A certain amount of fear and anxiety is necessary in life to protect us from danger or threats. This was critical 200,000 years ago for early humans. Since we first developed the capacity for thinking and language, we have made up stories, created religions, offered sacrifices, developed superstitions, and worshipped deities in a futile attempt to explain the inexplicable and control future events to quell our anxieties.

Throughout evolutionary history, we have lived with fear and anxiety. They are an inescapable aspect of being human and have been essential to our survival as a species – as a critical alarm system – as is the case for all creatures. The Buddha recognized fear and anxiety as part of the common human experience. Worry and restlessness – in other words, anxiety – is one of the five hindrances that the Buddha taught.

Since being anxiety-free is not possible, our challenge now is to manage fear and anxiety skillfully. We do not have to worry about the same physical threats to our survival that our ancestors did. Yes, real threats still exist in our modern world. Yet we need to find ways not to be consumed by fear or anxiety when it arises in response to imagined threats or an uncertain future. Practical dharma offers us the tools to do so. The dharma teaches we can change our relationship with fear and anxiety and, thereby, reduce the suffering they cause. The process begins with not seeing the experience as a weakness, or something about which to be ashamed. This includes not seeing fear and anxiety as enemies. The most effective psychotherapy methods for dealing with anxiety require that we lean into our anxieties and meet them head-on. We do not try to avoid them as this only worsens them and constricts our world.

What I say to individuals suffering from anxiety disorders is, 'don't get into a wrestling match with your anxiety, as you will lose'. This method of facing our anxiety is known as graduated exposure. It aligns with the Buddha's teachings on accepting all experience rather than avoiding that which is unpleasant. Using graduated exposure, we are exposed incrementally to that which we have avoided in the past out of anxiety. The way we can face our anxieties is broken down into small manageable increments or steps so we are not overwhelmed with anxiety or panic. The incremental steps are often done using imagination before moving on to live situations.

Anxiety and its close cousins come in many forms, including worry, rumination, impending doom, physical anxiety, panic, anxious anticipation, and a range of physical symptoms. All these manifestations have arousal of the nervous system's sympathetic branch in common: fight, flight, or freeze. Feeling anxiety and fear is something we all experience as part of the human journey. We each have different relationships with fear and anxiety, ranging from easy acceptance to total paralysis.

To be precise, we need to make a distinction between fear and anxiety. When there is a specific immediate threat or object about which we are afraid such as a noise in the dark, an immediate danger, the outcome of a negative medical test, or a truck veering into our lane we feel fear in response to that trigger. Fear occurs in real time. Anxiety, which has the same physiological manifestations as fear, is anticipatory. It is about future events and includes non-specific threats. We become anxious about growing older, our children getting hurt, becoming ill, dying, financial ruin, our marriage lasting, and a host of other concerns. Our capacity for imagination and language provides endless opportunities for anxiety from the stories we create. With anxiety, there is no current real-time specific object of alarm. Instead, we are responding to frailty, uncertainty, and the temporary nature of existence with anxiety. We project into the future, responding to our inability to predict or control it. The nature of impermanence that Gotama taught underlies all such anxieties.

To change our relationship with anxiety, we need to give up

the fantasy that we will ever be absolutely safe or have absolute control. The Buddha taught that all things are constantly changing and eventually disappear – even that which is most precious to us. Loss, great and small, constantly happens despite our resistance. This knowledge motivates us to plan and take sensible precautions about future risks, such as wearing a seat belt or getting a Covid vaccination, while of necessity giving up our efforts to control or predict the future – or holding onto the belief that we can avoid all future danger or loss.

As we gain more experience of spiritual practice, we inevitably encounter anxieties some of which we did not know were within us. This often happens when we become quiet during meditation. Anxieties can then become fuel for our practice and, in fact, are potential teachers on our path. Being alert and curious about our anxieties allows them to function as stimuli for us to notice. There are ways in which anxiety may be understood for us to work with it mindfully.

We may habitually view the world through the lens of our anxieties, such that we are living an anxiety-based life. There is very little mental rest when this is true because life seldom seems even temporarily safe. We continually mistrust our judgment, or we question the reliability of others. Constant worry about the future plagues us. Often we second-guess ourselves and others, continually seeking just one more opinion, or assurance. When existence is anxiety based, we tend to move from one obsession or worry to another. We are rarely able to be present in the moment. The only solution lies in changing our relationship with our anxieties.

Early in my practice of the dharma, I discovered that much of my daily behavior was motivated by anxiety. This included anxiety about failure, anxiety about disapproval, anxiety about disappointing others, anxiety about being judged negatively, and even anxiety about being anxious. The anxieties were present for most of my waking existence, which was exhausting and demoralizing; the source of much suffering. I suffered until I moved more deeply into the dharma. When I began practicing daily sitting meditation, the awareness of how much of my life was anxiety-based became apparent. What was also clear to me was how much shame I felt about being anxious, a situation that resulted from wanting to hide my anxiety from others. This only exacerbated my anxiety as I was also worried about being exposed as an anxious person, a common experience in a judging culture that expects perfection.

Anxiety is subjective; it happens inside us. Except in its most extreme forms, it is invisible to others. Given that it is subjective and internal how do we learn to live with it? The more established our mindfulness practice, the less likely we are to escalate from apprehension to heightened anxiety, and then panic and terror. We learn to be fully present with it as we do with any other experience. We cease identifying with it as part of our sense of self, as in, 'I am an anxious person'. Instead, we defuse it and label it as we would any other transient experience, 'anxiety is happening now' or 'anxiety is like this now'. We learn to lean into it, and face it head-on. Though we do not like it, we accept it and avoid getting into a wrestling match with it. The least skillful responses to anxiety are attempting to avoid it, suppress it, or distract from it because doing so only makes it worse.

One of the values of spiritual practice is that we can come to terms with our anxieties consciously. As the Buddha taught, we welcome all phenomena: pleasant, neutral, and unpleasant, of which anxiety is but one example. Our life becomes more integrated because we no longer try to deny or avoid what is true in the moment, even if uncomfortable like anxiety. We accept our anxieties without shame as just another common experience everyone experiences at some point.

Often, though, we compound the misery of the specific anxiety we are experiencing with the general anxiety inherent in the human condition. Mindfulness practice allows us to see how the untrained mind is agitated by the human experience, including vague perceived threats to our existence – our very mortality. We gain tolerance for the unpleasantness of uncertainty and the naturalness of our imperfection and we consciously and openly accept impermanence.

Gotama asks us to develop confidence that life is what it is – we cannot know the future much less control it. We cannot, nor are we supposed to, miraculously fix or eliminate anxiety. Instead, we gain the insight that contentment and peace come from relating to life just as it is, anxiety included, not as we wish it to be. Once we accept it as unpleasant and part of the flow of human experience, suffering lessens and greater freedom ensues.

There is no place for magical or wishful thinking when dealing with anxiety. To paraphrase a popular expression, 'anxiety happens'. When it does, hypervigilance occurs and all of our senses are scanning our surroundings and our internal experience for perceived danger. Challenging responses will likely present themselves at some point in our meditation practice or in our life in response to anxiety. Yet because it is unpleasant, we try to distract the mind and avoid them. It has been my experience – personally, and as a psychologist and dharma teacher – that if we can simply be fully present with the uncomfortable experience it will eventually release its grip both physically and mentally, as do all impermanent phenomena. One of the gifts practical dharma has given me is the ability to accept my anxiety.

Working with anxiety involves benevolence and goodwill toward ourselves, otherwise known as self-compassion, in the face of whatever arises. Yes, we are anxious, but instead of fighting it we embrace and accept it rather than unskillfully fighting it physically or mentally. Doing so only creates more turmoil in our minds and more anxiety symptoms in our bodies. We remember that anxiety is simply what is happening in the moment and doesn't define who we are. Working skillfully with anxiety involves accepting whatever we are experiencing.

Neuroscience has provided us with ways with which to understand the brain activity that accompanies anxiety. When the amygdala, the brain's alarm system, senses a threat it responds in a split second to activate the flight, fight, or freeze response. The neocortex, the more highly evolved area of the brain where thinking occurs, is slower to come online in the face of a threat. The neocortex will try to make sense of the danger and evaluate it. We cannot think ourselves out of anxiety. We must address it at the source, which is the amygdala.

Often, we develop anxiety about our anxiety, meaning that we develop a fearful response to the internal physical cues that signal a heightened anxiety response. Trying to stop or escape these sensations is known as experiential avoidance and is responsible for many, if not most, anxiety disorders. The internal responses include a rapid heartbeat, subjective panicky feelings, and hyperventilation. Physical symptoms are accompanied by catastrophic thoughts ('I can't stand this – I am going to freak out') creating a cascade response. Our challenge is whether we can just be with it. Watch it arise and pass away. Face it head-on. Trust that this, too, shall pass. Achieve a sense of mastery when we have successfully stayed with the anxiety response until it resolves.

Exposure to what is fearful allows the brain, specifically the amygdala, to experience that which is producing anxiety and see that no harm actually comes to us. Graduated exposure systematically does this so that over time the amygdala becomes desensitized to the triggers which are causing anxiety, be they internal or external. Research in psychology tells us that without an exposure component it is difficult to manage our anxieties more skillfully.

Exposure by imagination and fantasy can be as effective as exposure to the actual trigger for our anxiety and is a well-accepted psychotherapeutic technique.

There is extensive psychological research and literature in schools of psychotherapy on graduated exposure and similar methods, a thorough exploration of which is beyond the scope of this book. For our purposes, one example is a person who is terrified of enclosed spaces such as elevators, a disorder known as claustrophobia. Typically, anxiety is the result of a fear of being trapped in a confined space, and is relatively common, affecting approximately 13% of the US population. A program of exposure would have the person voluntarily enter into increasingly smaller enclosed spaces gradually so as not to be overwhelmed with panic. As anxiety arises in an enclosed space it is noted ('anxiety is happening'), watched as it arises while accompanied by slow deep breaths. The person remains present with anxious feelings until they subside which they will. Nonetheless, a strong urge to escape or leave the space will arise as the person feels trapped. They are instructed to resist the urge to leave and to remind themself that they are in no danger despite what their thoughts and physical responses are telling them. Once the anxiety subsides, they can leave the situation with a sense of mastery and confidence.

I have not said a great deal in this chapter about noticing since anxiety and fear are hard to ignore. They grab our attention aggressively and force us to notice. The challenge to notice anxiety arising is insignificant as it may be screaming in our face. At those moments, the challenge is to produce a skillful response to anxiety which includes accepting it, being fully present with it, leaning into it, welcoming it, and watching it as it arises and passes away. Finally, we avoid self-judgment or shame for having anxiety. We remember that persistent anxiety is a sign that we are fighting it and not accepting it.

Reflection

✦ How critically do you judge yourself when you experience anxiety? What do you imagine would happen if you simply accepted your anxiety?

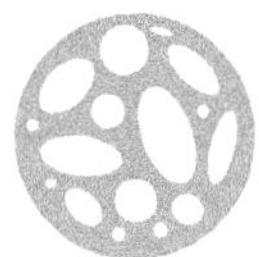

9. Cultivating patience

Do you have the patience to wait until your mud settles and the water is clear?
Laozi

It would be difficult to put practical dharma to use without cultivating patience, one of the ten perfections the Buddha taught. The perfections are virtues that we cultivate to live a life unobstructed by suffering. They are typically referred to by Buddhists as 'qualities of noble people'. Of the ten, patience is of particular importance. For a deeper exploration of all of the perfections, please refer to the references at the end of the book.

Patience is the ability to endure difficult circumstances with equanimity. It is perseverance when confronted with obstacles and tolerating provocation without reactivity. Patience is forbearance when we are faced with chronic challenges. It is a virtue in most of the world's faith traditions, while impatience is an obstacle to spiritual advancement and reduced suffering.

Impatience is a cause of much suffering and is typically marked by one or more of the following: anxiety ('am I in the right line?'), anger ('I don't have time for this'), envy ('I should be first;

it's my turn'), ego needs ('what about me?'), or other negative mood states.

An impatient state of mind cannot co-exist with being fully present and awake as it is a barrier to present-moment awareness. Instead, we focus on the frustration we feel about a pending occurrence or obstacle.

Strictly speaking, the Buddhist concept of patience differs from the English definition of the word. In Buddhism, patience refers to refraining from returning harm, not just enduring a difficult situation. It is not just a frame of mind but is also about our behavior when confronted with a situation that tests our patience. It is the ability to control one's emotions and behavior even when criticized or attacked. It is also characterized as a form of non-reactivity.

We cultivate patience because we seek both inward and outward peace. It is a function of our ability to accept things as they are in the moment. To return to the earlier example of being stuck in traffic, I can let impatience take over with all the attendant suffering or I can accept that there is nothing I can do other than be present with the fact that traffic is not moving. Simply put, whenever we want life to be different than it is we experience impatience; so we suffer. We lose our sense of humor and indulge in self-pity. Despair, blame, and resentment arise in us as nothing changes with the situation in which we find ourselves and the frustrating circumstances persist.

Patience plays an important role in our relationships. Acceptance, compassion, and forgiveness are often lacking when impatience prevails in our relationships. What we fail to recognize in dealing with others is that bringing patient understanding (compassion) to the other person's challenges and their suffering is the first step to being able to communicate, forgive, and begin anew.

The practice of forgiveness and acceptance happens when

we realize the underlying cause of our anger and impatience. Doing so requires discernment about the other person's unskillful behavior as we understand it and see their essential goodness. Serenity and calm develop as we accept the unskillful aspects of others and ourselves. This does not mean that we tolerate being mistreated. Setting clear boundaries with those who seek to hurt or exploit us is wise action. Discernment is the tool that guides us toward wise action when we encounter a toxic interpersonal situation.

There are three components to cultivating patience. The first is forbearance, followed by calm endurance of hardship, and finally, acceptance of the truth as it is.

Gentle forbearance is not the same as acceptance of how things are. But it is no less critical as it inhibits our speaking or acting long enough to determine the most skillful course of action, given that with which we are dealing. It is putting in a sacred pause before we respond.

The second aspect of patience is enduring hardship with calm equanimity. We must remember that the Buddha taught that the world 'rests on suffering'. Yet, we do not passively endure suffering and do nothing to lessen it as though we have no agency as individuals. Here again, discernment guides us on how to endure or respond to hardship and reduce our suffering. Patience is not passive. It signals us to accept and feel compassion for all the suffering while recognizing that we cannot eradicate it and can only reduce it. When we feel impatient in our lives, relationships, job or spiritual path, we are resisting how things truly are. Noticing impatience is the cue to let go of resistance and relax into the situation as it is.

I find that humor and curiosity about what is going on at moments of impatience help me manage challenges more skillfully. At those moments impatience manifests both in our thoughts and physical response, and serves as a red flag. In such situations, it helps to ask, 'what would being patient look like right now?'. We use present moment awareness to explore what happens with the relationship to our experience at those times. When we do so, relief, gratitude and contentment often follow, especially when we are rushing around trying to anticipate what is next.

In our over-stimulated, multitasking, gadget-obsessed, social media era, we are doing so many things at once that there is little space for serenity or patience. Yet, we wonder why we are unhappy and feel alienated. The challenge we have is to remember, several times a day, to practice relaxing into life with all its joys and sorrows, and relinquish the need to know what will happen next.

The third aspect of patience requires that we accept our experience as it is rather than how we want it to be. Our experience is continually changing due to impermanence so we know it will change if only we have patience. Accepting things as they are requires noticing and discernment, profound wisdom, and compassion. These take time to cultivate. We are then less likely to get caught in being overly insistent, frustrated, and demanding, all of which are the wellspring of impatience and the resulting suffering.

Another benefit of patience is that it cuts through arrogance, entitlement, and ingratitude, and lessens the power of the ego. When we think that we are the center of the universe, impatience results when the world gets in the way. Patience helps us cultivate humility, a characteristic that moves us from resistance to acceptance, spontaneous presence, and patience. We relax and see the suffering diminish.

Holding onto our judgments about others and ourselves is a significant cause of impatience and suffering. By accepting both the pleasant and unpleasant aspects of life, including the behavior of those to whom we are close, we cease wishing for life to be other than it is. We are freer of the demands that we constantly put on ourselves and others which are dominated by feelings of impatience. As a result, we are awake for all of life on its terms, not ours.

Do not confuse patience with passivity, reticence, or procrastination, which are qualities made of resistance, avoidance, and low energy. Patience is intentional and purposeful, and requires discernment and an intention to cultivate. It is best practiced in less challenging circumstances rather than in the heat of the moment, allowing us to learn the skills needed in more difficult situations.

Cultivating patience is no quick fix. It takes effort and requires a robust and long-term commitment. I am not saying that we do not see benefits along the way. Our ongoing work results in less suffering even though our efforts are never done. Westerners want instant transformation and instant gratification because we are culturally impatient. There is no easy response to the struggles we face in our lives. The methods of practical dharma are slow, incremental and cumulative, and require an ongoing commitment. Without patience, the inclination is to abandon the practice. This is why it is such an important part of the path.

I frequently notice, or a loved one observes, that I am responding skillfully and with more patience to challenging situations that used to cause me and those around me much suffering. Such change is gradual, usually appearing when we are not expecting it. The rewards of reduced suffering and greater freedom from cultivating patience are well worth the effort. We must work at it and pursue it with the intention to change as it will not fall in our laps. Practical dharma is not a set of passive practices where transformation happens simply from sitting in meditation every day. We must set an intention to implement the tools available to us in our daily lives for changes to occur.

Let us briefly review the enemies of patience. We start where we often do with the ego. Arrogance and a sense of entitlement, born of the ego, are attitudes in which a lack of patience is embedded. Though neither is the same as anger they are closely related.

Impatience is a typical response to anger, waiting in the wings to arise when we are frustrated or thwarted. The hurry-up sickness and sense of urgency that is pervasive in our culture is ripe ground for impatience.

Who suffers when we are impatient with others? True, the person we find frustrating may suffer if we react to them but, primarily, we suffer. Can we use the suffering that comes from our impatience as a teacher? To remind us to address it skillfully with the tools available to us?

Equanimity, which is one of the Buddha's four immeasurables, helps us cultivate patience. As with every aspect of our practice, we begin with noticing followed by the pause and tuning into bodily reactions that characterize impatience as our cues. We become aware when impatience arises, noting what it feels like and where it is occurring in the body. Accompanying thought patterns and stories, which will feel idiosyncratic, predictable, and familiar to us, are additional cues. We are now halfway toward managing our impatience more skillfully since we are fully and consciously aware of it. Once we notice, and see clearly with insight and discernment the sources of our impatience, we pause and breathe. We then give ourselves the directive to consciously let go of what we are holding onto that is feeding our impatience.

All the tools of our practice as well as the steps of the eightfold path involve, either directly or indirectly, the cultivation of patience. Patient people are happy people. I am more at peace when I am patient, as you will be.

Reflection

✦ Think about the situations that predictably make you impatient. Is it because someone is not responding to your expectations? What other triggers can you identify?

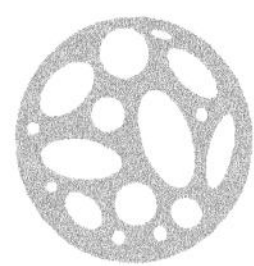

10. Judging and comparison

Comparison is the thief of joy.
Teddy Roosevelt

Teddy Roosevelt sums up an important dilemma, and a source of suffering that we all face daily on the dharma path: comparing ourselves to others while we judge them – both of which are unavoidable tendencies.

We compare anything and everything about ourselves – our behavior, our income, our mental health, our attractiveness, our relationships, our possessions, our status, our homes, our pets, and on and on. The result of all this comparing and self-judging is increased suffering.

Comparisons and judgments are going on constantly in the background even when we are not fully conscious of them. Now that everyone's life is on social media, there has been an explosion of comparing. A recent product of social media is known as FOMO: fear of missing out. With FOMO, we judge our social lives. We try to determine if others are having more fun, leading more exciting lives, or going to more social functions. This modern phenomenon is one of many that has increased the suffering that comparing and judging creates.

Evolutionary psychology tells us that we are hard-wired to compare ourselves to others. The technical term for this is status-watching. Human thinking patterns evolved to detect our physical, social, and intellectual differences from others. The shame-pride continuum, as well as access to the best food and breeding opportunities are involved in the process.

Social psychology reveals that when we use comparing to try to make ourselves feel better, we compare ourselves to people we perceive as having lower status. Alternatively, when we imagine our status is low, we look to people of higher status for clues about what we should aspire to in order to increase our status. If an individual's status is high or rising, they take steps to fend off rivals. High status engenders pride, an inflated sense of self, and respect from peers, all of which are ego-driven. On the other end of the continuum, the shame of low status creates feelings of inferiority, vulnerability, and fear of rejection.

Most species that function in groups have a pecking order, or hierarchical group structure. We humans have pecking orders, comparing ourselves and judging others as a vestige of our human evolution.

We live in a competitive culture where status is determined by wealth, possessions, educational attainment, attractiveness, and winning. Motivating much of the pursuit is comparing, which often results in ongoing self-criticism. We struggle to 'keep up with the Joneses' and judge ourselves failures if we fall behind our neighbors in these areas, generating more suffering. The dharma offers tools for lessening this distress.

Children are not born with comparing minds. Their brains are not sufficiently developed to respond other than to sensations of hunger, elimination, temperature and comfort. As the child's brain develops it is exposed to a competitive culture hundreds of thousands of years in the making. Cultural norms get internalized by the child. Comparisons such as safe/unsafe and tasteful/toxic are necessary for a child's survival and are usually the first categories of comparison for a young child.

The process expands during childhood fed by cultural messages and developing peer relationships. Cultural norms become more complex until by early adolescence teens are in full-on comparing mode. For this reason, adolescence is a very challenging time for teens. It is why peer pressure is so powerful and everything – including experiences, clothing choices, appearances, friend choices, winning, losing, popularity, and family status – is grist for the mill of comparison. The underlying threats of shame, unpopularity, and feeling inadequate are ever-present. Teens will take significant risks, sometimes fatal, to achieve or preserve high status. If we survive our teen years, we bring into adulthood the template for a life of comparing and judging.

Advertisers and marketers exploit our comparing tendencies by convincing us that if we only drive the right car, wear the right clothes, and drink the right beer we will surpass others in a never-ending pursuit of status. The role of 'influencers' is a recent phenomenon in our culture. People with large social media followings who are hired by companies to showcase their wares. What brand of sneakers are influencers wearing? What car are they driving? What brands of clothing do they wear? Being 'cool' requires that we emulate the influencer, is the intended message.

We seek and then cling and grasp to those things we believe will bring us status, and therefore happiness. We create stories and narratives to support our pursuits. But it is a fool's errand and an endless futile quest because of the law of impermanence. We are on a treadmill from which we can never escape if we do not take steps to intervene with intention.

My college years were characterized by judging and comparing mind. I believed my worth to be a function of my status when compared to my peers. It was critical that I attend the right college, join the right fraternity, date attractive women from the right women's colleges, drive the right car, wear the most fashionable clothes, and go to the best parties. Though I did well academically (in part to avoid being drafted and sent to Viet Nam), grades were secondary to my social life. I firmly believed that if I did everything right concerning status, I would finally be happy. However, I never was happy because someone else always outdid me in the categories I deemed important. I led a hollow and meaningless existence, not that I let anyone know in case my suffering be exposed and ridiculed.

What tools does the dharma offer that enable us to manage our comparing minds more skillfully and reduce our suffering? Noticing with mindful awareness where we are getting hooked is first, as is often the case. Noticing how often we compare ourselves and judge others, and the forms it takes. Seeing how comparing results in competition with, and envy of, others, we begin to see how we feel inflated but vulnerable when we are winning, and deflated when we are losing. The suffering accompanies each of these. We notice that we worry about losing if we are winning, and feeling like a failure when losing.

Second, as we become aware we label it with a simple reminder to ourselves such as 'comparing mind' or 'judging mind'. Labeling opens the door to let go of the comparison and rein in the ego's need to compete, win, and feel superior to others. I find it tremendously helpful at moments like these to practice compassion for myself, along with those with whom I have been comparing myself.

Another one of the four immeasurables is practicing sympathetic joy. This is the taking of pleasure in someone else's good fortune, a powerful antidote to envying those with whom we feel less than. Doing so lessens the ego's power over our feelings in those moments, and reduces our suffering.

Such practices broaden our perspective and create a sense of spaciousness which puts comparing in a larger context. We experience equanimity and are less reactive. When we are not in comparing mode, we are more open and available for meaningful connection with others regardless of their perceived status. We manage envy, jealousy, and competition more skillfully. Contrary to what Teddy Roosevelt said, our joy is no longer stolen; it has become available to us.

Reduced competition and envy open the door for more meaningful connection with others. Such emotional intimacy is an antidote for loneliness, isolation, negative self-judgment, and acceptance of all of who we are. It is one of the joys that life offers us – so long as we avail ourselves of it. It is yet another experience for which we can feel gratitude for this path.

Reflection

✦ Are you able to see where your self-worth, how you feel about yourself, is tied to comparing yourself to others or an external standard?

III • SEE REACTIVITY STOP

In this section, we introduce a rationale for practicing the dharma and revisit aspects of the roadmap for beginning to lessen our suffering; the emphasis here is on recognizing and reducing, or eliminating, habitual reactions to life's challenges.

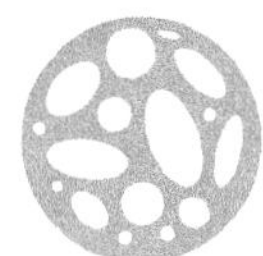

11. Why we practice the dharma

Joy arises when we stop striving to be different and instead appreciate who we already are.

Martine Batchelor

Let's consider the question of why we follow the path that Gotama offered us. The primary gift of the dharma is that it helps us to reduce our suffering and live a more fulfilling life without having to resort to truth claims or belief in the supernatural. As Buddhist practitioners, we are often caricatured as being obsessed with suffering. It is true that we focus on suffering but we do so as a means to reduce it. We do not stop there, though. We actively cultivate greater joy in our lives. Indeed, suffering and joy could be said to be two sides of the same coin: when we choose to decrease our experience of suffering, we create the conditions to experience more joy.

Reducing suffering was Gotama's main intention – his main goal for his followers. He is quoted in the suttas as having said: 'I teach suffering and the end of suffering'. Of course, he did not mean that we get through this life without suffering. He was not referring to the unavoidable forms of suffering – illness, old age, death, and loss. Rather, he was alluding to the aspect of our suffering over which we have agency, that is, how we respond to it. Because how we respond to any experience significantly shapes the experience itself; it has the potential to worsen or lessen our suffering.

Modern psychology uses terms such as emotional resilience, emotional intelligence, and psychological flexibility to describe qualities that support us to live a more joyful life. These are different terms for what is essentially the same style of interacting with the world: one in which we are able to take responsibility for ourselves, our behaviors, and our reactions, regardless of the external conditions that may be influencing our lives. (Often, these terms are used interchangeably; for the purpose of this book, we'll use emotional resilience to describe this state.)

The achievement of emotional resilience, which can also be characterized as a state of non-reactivity is, in my view as a psychologist, the strongest argument for practicing the dharma. I believe it to be the most direct means of lessening the experience of suffering and increasing the experience of joy. In this chapter, we will review some of the key components of the dharma that teach and support us as we loosen our grip on causes of suffering, thereby opening our hearts to greater joy.

A large part of practicing the Buddha's teachings is that it helps us to relinquish the delusions – those self-serving beliefs that we hold on to even as they contradict reality – that cause us, and those close to us, so much suffering. We need to cultivate emotional resilience if we are going to be able to deal realistically and constructively with reality – to be with what is – free of harmful delusions, distortions, or what might be called our own 'spin'.

In terms of the dharma, this means seeing things as they truly are, not as we wish them to be. This is much easier said than done because we bring our biases, our prejudices, our early learning, our cultural influences, and many other 'lenses' to bear on how we perceive the world – most of which are invisible to us to begin with. Addressing this same dynamic is central to most modern psychotherapy.

I spent years telling myself that I was a nice person and that any behavior I might display to the contrary was always the fault of whomever or whatever had provoked me. For a long time, it was too painful for me to admit the reality that I was an angry, controlling person. My ego did not want to hear this! But once I began to practice the dharma and get to grips with the four tasks, I found my way to getting more comfortable with what was happening, instead of what I wanted to believe about myself and others. Eventually I was able to take a really cold, hard look at myself, and when I did, I could no longer maintain the delusion that I was a good person while I was treating others poorly.

From a Buddhist perspective, we attain emotional resilience by accepting that the true nature of all things is impermanence. Impermanence is an inarguable aspect of what is: it is simply a fact that everything within us and outside us is in a state of constant change. It sounds so simple, and yet it can be one of the hardest things for a person to accept.

Accepting impermanence requires that we accept the fact that nothing lasts forever; that everything is in a constant state of flux. This is often the last thing we want to hear, because doing so requires that we admit that, contrary to our wishes, we are not in control. Things such as illness, the weather, world events, and how others respond to us are just a few of the facts of life that are always in flux, and which we will never be able to control. If and when we find we can come to accept this existentially terrifying prospect, a whole new horizon of questions and invitations opens up. Knowing that life is constantly changing, can we adapt to it? Can we flow with it, or will we hunker down and try to deny it, applying even more force in an attempt to control it?

A critical aspect of embracing impermanence is becoming comfortable with uncertainty and accepting our inability to control the future: accepting that aside from what I had for breakfast this morning, I cannot control much of what transpires in my life today. Resisting or denying impermanence, trying to control things over which I have no control, is a large source of suffering.

The practice of equanimity, which is the ability to withstand the changing winds of life, is another central tenet of dharma practice that, when practiced effectively, supports us in remaining grounded during difficult circumstances – in other words, to not get 'knocked over' by the shifting circumstances of life. With the practice of equanimity, we cultivate the ability to experience moments of suffering without intense reactivity and with minimal disturbance.

We learn to practice equanimity by 'rolling with the punches', and in doing so we become ever less likely to be thrown off balance by prevailing winds; we stay grounded regardless of what life throws at us. It is a way of relating to the world that recognizes its ever-changing nature, and the futility of attempting to apply force of will where it is useless.

One quality to which the Buddha gave a lot of weight is generosity: the capacity to find more satisfaction in giving than in receiving. This is found in most faith traditions. As the Bible's New Testament puts it, 'It is more blessed to give than to receive'.

Generosity, by its very nature, chips away at self-centeredness. It challenges the egoic desires that always center around me. When we give without expectation of reward, our generosity becomes its own reward, and as a result we loosen the grip of ego.

Next is the ability to relate openly and honestly to others without intense emotional reactivity. From a dharma perspective, this aligns with the teachings of loving-kindness, compassion, sympathetic joy, and equanimity – the four immeasurables. Practicing the four immeasurables is the path to relating openly and honestly with others, with minimal reactivity. We learn to 'walk in the other person's shoes'. We bring a spaciousness to our interactions rather than the tunnel vision of our ego which is characterized by thoughts such as, 'I've got to win', 'I've got to prevail', or 'I've got to be top dog'.

Cognitive defusion is a concept in modern psychology that refers to changing the undesirable functions of our thoughts and other internal experiences such as emotions, sensations, and mental narratives that are harmful to our sense of well-being. In dharma terms, this means not becoming identified with the stories we tell ourselves, and not believing everything we think. As the Buddha taught, we recognize that there is no fixed self, despite what the ego tries to tell us. Our identity, our preferences, our intentions, all change moment to moment. We come to understand that we are not our stories, our emotions, our physical sensations – especially the ones which cause us much suffering. We are in fact the awareness that witnesses all these things yet remains untouched by them.

Finally, and to come full circle with the first practice of being with what is, developing emotional resilience requires us to live mindfully in the moment: to be fully present not just with what is, but also to whatever our experience of what is may be at any time. This is the present moment awareness that Gotama taught in the four foundations of mindfulness. We do not dwell on past regrets or focus on the 'what ifs' of the future. To the best of our ability, we live in the moment.

One of my dharma teachers once said to me, 'if we're living in the past or focused on the future, by definition, we're suffering'. While this is a simplification, it is unequivocally true: to live in the past is to be licking our wounds over past regrets; to obsess over the future is in some way an attempt to control the future, both of which lead to suffering. So, the present moment is another antidote to suffering.

Modern psychology and neuroscience have rediscovered what the Buddha understood 2400 years ago: the nature of suffering, where it manifests in the brain, and the antidotes for it. Gotama's dharma offers immense rewards, including a more spiritual life, a more joyful life, and a life with significantly reduced suffering. I know of no other path, no other school of thought, nor any other faith tradition that offers so many benefits – if we're willing to put in the time and effort.

Reflection

✦ In what ways can the practice of generosity lead to a deeper sense of fulfillment and detachment from ego-driven desires in your life? How might cultivating equanimity and present moment awareness transform your response to life's inevitable changes and uncertainties?

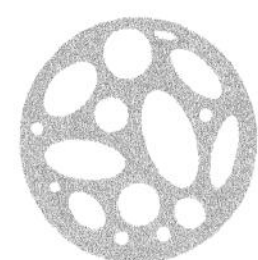

12. Noticing and mindful awareness

You may even have so many thoughts that it seems as if trying to meditate makes them increase, but you are just noticing the previously unidentified extent of your own ramblings. Your attempts at mindfulness are causing you to notice what is happening.

Tenzin Gyatso, the 14th Dalai Lama

One important practice I always include in my teaching is the fundamental activity of noticing. If we are on autopilot and not mindful and noticing experience, we cannot utilize the other tools of our practice. We must actively seek contact with the present moment.

Once we undertake the practice of noticing, we develop the habit of pausing when we are in a challenging situation. This is sufficiently important that we can refer to it as the 'sacred pause'.

Noticing is an essential part of being mindful. For example, if I am in a long slow checkout line at the supermarket and begin to feel irritated, that is a cue to notice what is going on internally. I pause to pay attention to where I feel out of sorts in the body. What thoughts are arising? What story am I telling myself about the line taking so long? What steps can I take to change my perspective and create spaciousness around what is happening? Doing so creates an opportunity to let go of the self-centered, ego-based, expectation that the line should move faster for me.

The process is not as complicated or involved as it sounds; typically, it only takes a couple of moments. We simply shift our attention to the body. Is there tightness or tension? Where in the body? Is our jaw clenched? Can we feel frustration or irritation arising in our midsection? What unskillful thoughts are accompanying the changes in our body?

Noticing and pausing open the door to reducing suffering in the form of frustration and impatience, such as driving in slow traffic. Situations like this present an opportunity for acceptance of a situation as it is, where we let go of our expectations and sense of self-importance. Imagine what it can do for more challenging situations, especially in the relationship realm.

Another critical and related skill is discernment. This is a close cousin of noticing, and is the process of differentiating between beneficial and not beneficial choices in whatever context we find ourselves. Discernment involves seeing life clearly without delusion, not as we want it to be. Discernment is a critical step in pointing to where we need to let go of clinging or attachments that cause suffering. It is also essential to our ethical foundation and the development of wisdom.

The Buddha suggested that we seek out wise contemplatives to help with discernment. This is why working with a teacher on this path can be beneficial. We all have blind spots as we travel the path of the dharma, and a wise teacher can help us identify them. Having a teacher also helps to tame the ego by reinforcing a position of humility. Over the years, the guidance of my teacher has been critically important to my journey on the Buddhist path.

Gotama stated that the search for real long-term happiness

could only succeed if we employ discernment in our lives. We have agency over our decisions and choices – we only need to exercise them skillfully. Discernment helps us see if our decisions are wholesome or unwholesome and whether they will lead to more suffering or a reduction in suffering.

The notion of karma found in ancestral Buddhism is a vestige of Hinduism, and refers to cycles of death and birth. Secular Buddhists eschew this notion. For many western Buddhists, it has been replaced with the idea that actions have consequences. This is the law of cause and effect, often characterized as 'what goes around, comes around'. Or, as the Holy Bible says, 'as ye sow, so shall ye reap'. When we engage in meritorious acts we reap the rewards of inner satisfaction, extending goodwill to others, and making the world better. The Buddha taught that our actions and choices are impactful, so we should be mindful of that fact and use discernment and wisdom to guide us.

Discernment can also help us delay gratification when pursuing sensual pleasure. Gotama considered sensual pleasure one of the five hindrances that hold us back on our path. All five hindrances (sensual desire, ill-will, doubt, sloth and torpor, and restlessness/worry) are considered habits of mind that disrupt our meditation practice, and progress on the path. Anything that impinges on our senses, what Gotama called 'sense doors', can become a hindrance to our present-moment awareness if we fail to manage it skillfully.

Discernment helps us distinguish between healthy and unhealthy desires. Unchecked desire can turn into a compulsion or addiction, interfere with our awareness of the present moment, and create problems in our relationships and lives. As we bring discernment to our desires, we may find they are tied to ideas about emotional connection, security, success, status, or a need for reassurance. Are we trying to use sense pleasures to fill an emotional void such as sadness or loneliness? If so, we have to understand desire as 'an itch that can't be scratched'. Discernment is the tool needed to make such distinctions.

In my years of practice as a clinical psychologist, I found that desire and craving for sense pleasures were for many people an attempt to self-medicate unpleasant emotional states, an example of experiential avoidance. These include eating when not hungry, seeking casual or compulsive sex, intoxication with drugs or alcohol, compulsive spending, excessive gambling, spending hours on the internet, compulsive exercise or, indeed, anything done to excess that takes us away from being in the present moment. Noticing, pausing, and discernment are the means of beginning to manage problematic desires more skillfully.

We often reach for a habitual source of comfort for our ills when we are tired, sad, stressed, or overwhelmed. While doing so temporarily distracts us from an unpleasant feeling state, it prevents us from dealing with our mood more skillfully. The feeling state persists. At that moment we are not pausing, noticing, or using discernment. This is how addiction or compulsion pulls us toward sensual pleasure. Often it is a misplaced attempt to fill an emotional emptiness or manage frustration or other negative emotional state.

With mindfulness, present-moment focus, and being open to all experience, we learn to fill our inner emotional emptiness with awareness, spaciousness, and a sense of connection to everything and everyone. When we become familiar with our tendency to look for sensual desire by noticing, pausing, and discernment, freedom only requires looking at desire directly, naming it, and feeling how it is experienced in the body.

If I do not reach for chocolate but instead bring mindful awareness to my unpleasant mood, I have the option to address the mood skillfully. I can then touch into the joy of being present, settled, and concentrated. Sensual desire becomes less and less powerful. The satisfaction and confidence I experience then helps me manage the compulsion behind the desire. As we become free of the compulsive desire for sensual pleasure by pausing, noticing, and discerning, we use that freedom to decide wisely which desires and aspirations we will allow to guide our life.

Another aspect of noticing is shining a flashlight into the dark corners of who we are by taking a brutally honest look at ourselves, especially our unwholesome and problematic personality traits and behavior patterns. We are all capable of denying or disavowing the parts of ourselves that we feel to be harmful, unacceptable, or contrary to how we like to view ourselves – the parts we feel so ashamed about that we deny, or hide. Acknowledging them is a complex process as our ego screams, 'No, no, no, don't make me look'.

I am describing what the Swiss psychoanalyst, Carl Jung, called 'the shadow self'. He characterized it as composed of repressed ideas, instincts, impulses, weaknesses, desires, perversions, and shameful and embarrassing fears. It is often the wellspring of our reactivity, suffering, and poor choices.

Note that discerning does not involve judging. Judging ourselves in the process of noticing or discerning causes contraction and shame, not freedom and openness.

Reflection

✦　Noticing practice requires a significant shift from our usual way of functioning on autopilot. What challenges do you foresee in beginning a noticing practice?

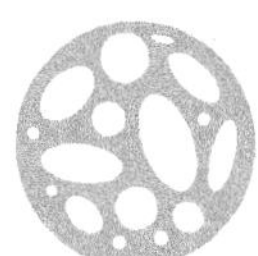

13. Finding calm in overwhelm

Real wisdom is recognizing and accepting that every experience is impermanent. With this insight you will not be overwhelmed by ups and downs.

S.N. Goenka

There are many times on this human journey that can be challenging and difficult. This is why many of us go to a sangha. The challenges come in many forms that test our strength and resilience – disappointments, setbacks, misfortunes, losses, and disasters. Too often, we are ill-prepared for these challenges. In the midst of them, we wonder if we even have the strength to cope.

None of us are spared this experience of feeling vulnerable, afraid and overwhelmed, past or present. When it happens, our instinctual response may be to lose focus, respond with less than skillful means, or freeze. We default to well honed, automated, reflexive habits that may help us feel better momentarily – primarily through avoidance – but which do not serve us well in the long term. We may know that avoidance is only a temporary solution; however, if we do all we can to escape or avoid what's happening to us, no new skills or coping mechanisms are learned, and we remain just as unprepared for the next crisis. This knowledge alone is not always enough for us to make a different choice.

Despite my knowledge and experience from being a practicing psychologist for over 45 years and following the dharma path for 35 years, I still get overwhelmed at times, as we all do. I am not immune to getting knocked off balance when I am triggered into reactivity by some challenging situation. As is true for all of us, I am always going to be, for the rest of my days, a work in progress. This awareness simply reminds me that the struggle to stay grounded is part of normal human experience. In no way does it indicate that we are weak or ineffective. We are not broken or defective when we struggle with crises or challenges – we are human beings, and this is part of the human experience.

But what if we had a go-to, pre-arranged, dharma-informed strategy that we could reach for whenever intense emotions or crisis situations threaten to overwhelm us? This would certainly make a difference to our experience! Fortunately, there is one. It is laid out for us to follow, and I lay it out here for you in the most simple terms.

The first step, as is so often the case, is our old friend, noticing. When the world seems to be crashing around us, our instinct is typically to react. In fact, the best way forward is simply to do nothing other than notice what is happening. Noticing invites us to get curious, to come at our discomfort with fresh eyes and beginners' mind.

If we have a history of avoiding uncomfortable feelings – as many of us do – this can be pretty scary. Our default is likely to be, 'I don't want to be here. I'd rather run away and distract myself'.

This is why the next important step is to ground. When we ground – for instance by taking a few slow breaths, orienting to the space around us rather than getting caught up in the workings of the mind, or doing any activity we enjoy that helps us feel calmer

– we create a greater sense of safety and capacity in the body and mind that allows us to respond to the situation consciously, rather than react to it unconsciously.

Once we have noticed and found a little bit more ground for ourselves, we can enter into step three, acknowledging. We can acknowledge that whatever is going on is difficult, and hard for us. We acknowledge the reactions that we are having – emotional, psychological, physical, and so on – without reacting to them in the way that we likely feel compelled to. We honor what is happening; 'I see that I don't want to be here. I see that I'd rather run away and distract myself'.

Next, we remind ourselves that we are not going to be swept away; we have the necessary tools, practices, and strategies to guide us. We remind ourselves that we can be with whatever is arising. We bring tools: kindness, patience, self-compassion, and grounding. Most importantly, we remember that whatever we're experiencing in the moment is impermanent. I see that I don't want to be here, and offer myself compassion, kindness, and patience as I weather these uncomfortable feelings. I see that I'd rather run away and distract myself. I can recollect that I have the tools to care for myself, and that this discomfort is not permanent. I remember that this, too, shall pass.

Noticing, grounding, acknowledging, and reminding allows enough time to pass that we have created a pause between the 'cause' of the situation and the 'effect', our response. This in turn allows for the potential of a moment of clarity to arise in the midst of an otherwise highly charged emotional state. We find we are able to get curious as to a solution or way ahead without having to force or take an action from a state of panic or fear.

While this may sound easy, it is anything but. Our innate, instinctual tendency when faced with challenging situations is to avoid or evade by fighting, fleeing, or freezing. These are natural human survival responses that we share with many other creatures in the animal kingdom, and which kick in instinctively when we perceive danger. Depending on the nature of the threat, we may fight back. We may flee, or run away. We may freeze (think of a possum 'playing possum', pretending to be dead to deter a predator).

All of these states constitute forms of avoidance. In the appropriate circumstance, for instance real physical danger, each can prove a life-saving response. They have been honed over thousands of years of evolution, after all. But in many scenarios in our modern human lives, where we may perceive an abstract sense of threat – think of an unwelcome bill when money is tight, a nasty comment from a troll on the internet, or the conversation with a colleague that triggered you and which you can't seem to let go of – we unconsciously perceive immediate physical danger where in fact there is none.

When we are experiencing a crisis mindful awareness and intention enables us to notice a fight, flight, or freeze reaction, and choose to pause before taking action. This is why we practice mindfulness regularly, as a natural part of our meditation practice, in less charged situations: to help us 'build the muscle' of awareness that allows us to create space between our experiences and our reactions to them.

Over time, this practice builds the mental muscle memory we will need to be able to recall it and apply it during times of acute stress. If we do not have this 'muscle memory', we will most likely lose ourselves in the commotion of our inner thoughts and feelings when we feel we are being hammered by a situation.

In contrast, when we begin to hone the skillset of mindful noticing, we find we are able to watch our experiences from a greater distance, observing the thoughts and feelings and physical and emotional urges to react as they unfold in the present moment, without the same intensity of panic and fear and reactivity we would otherwise. Only then can we move on skillfully.

This is the invitation with overwhelm. To notice our feelings as we experience them in the present moment, as quickly as possible, before they have the chance to escalate. This is what opens up a wider vista of possibilities for making conscious choices about what to do next – rather than just reacting reflexively with a dysfunctional default response. By not falling back on old strategies that are ineffective, we are able to instead make a conscious decision about how to proceed; we create the opportunity for ourselves to use skills of wisdom and discernment, rather than panic and avoidance, before responding. Not easy to do, it is invaluable to learn. Slow, deep, full breaths, with an emphasis on the exhale, are our most direct and powerful tool for 'down regulating' the fight-flight-freeze response of our nervous system and returning to a state of 'rest and digest'. This is why we use every small experience of charged emotion to practice honing this skillset. Over time we build our capacity and emotional resilience, and find ourselves better able to recall this practice when overwhelm threatens to overtake us.

During this process, any time that the intensity of our experience threatens to overwhelm us, we come back to grounding. Getting grounded in our bodies is what allows us to safely enter into the next step, which is to be present with what we're feeling. If we are not grounded, our experience is likely to become too overwhelming. So, in order to face the discomfort in a way that is supportive rather than more harmful, we ground. We can take a walk. Plant our feet on the ground. Drink a glass of water, write a text, or journal. Listen to our favorite music. Practice the breathing exercise in the paragraph above. Give our dogs a belly rub. Anything that allows us to orient outside of ourself in a way that lightens the intensity of our inner experience. Once we feel grounded – that is, a little bit calmer, and more present, and centered – it's time to return inward and attend.

The next step is to be present with our strong emotions as they arise. To begin with, this will likely feel impossible, because our default, evolutionary response when we feel overwhelmed, uncomfortable, or in pain is to run away, avoid, or distract ourselves as a means of separating ourselves from the unpleasant feelings. But this is a slippery slope. We might do anything we can to feel better – run away, distract ourselves, numb out by stuffing ourselves with comfort food, overspending when shopping online, or getting lost in social media, turn to alcohol or drugs to alleviate the stress, or lash out at others as a way of transferring responsibility or discharging the overwhelming sensations in our body. Any form of escapism we feel is available to us, especially when it feels familiar and/or we saw it modelled to us in childhood by our caregivers.

The problem with this kind of response is that while it may work for a while, it doesn't last. We gain no skills and we build no resilience when we avoid the overwhelm rather than addressing it. The next time we find ourselves overwhelmed, we repeat the same unhelpful pattern. We don't learn, we don't grow, we don't benefit, and we don't develop more skillful strategies.

On top of all of that, we continue to lean on unhealthy coping mechanisms that become increasingly more harmful over time. If not kept in check, we find we become more and more reliant on these 'tools' to escape our reality – and we need to increase our embrace of them to gain the same result. This is how addiction occurs, resulting in far greater suffering over time, as we grow more and more dependent on experiential avoidance behaviors that cause more and more harm over time. It becomes a very vicious cycle indeed.

This is why it is so important to remember that even when feeling overwhelmed, we still have choices. Just remembering that we have choices can be enough to begin to empower ourselves out of the kind of helplessness that feeds addiction and other avoidance strategies.

It takes time and courage to learn to simply be with uncomfortable feelings – to just sit with them, be present with them, and allow them to be what they are. Again, the task is mindful presence. Take a moment to check in with the body and check in with the thoughts. Where's the commotion? Where's the overwhelm manifesting in the body? Despite all the discomfort, is there a place in the body where we are perhaps still feeling steady? Can we ground ourselves despite the sensations? And what is happening with the breath?

The primary resource we have available to us for emotional regulation is the breath. If we are overwhelmed yet able to check in with our breathing, it's invariably going to be rapid and shallow, and is ramping up the sympathetic nervous system and increasing the sense of overwhelm. If we are able to notice what we are feeling, both emotionally and physically, and then slow down the breath in the face of that discomfort, we can soothe the nervous system and extricate ourselves from overwhelm. Practicing this kind of controlled breathing in our meditation practice daily is important, as it is a critical step in managing overwhelm.

When we are in the midst of overwhelm, it may seem like it is going to go on forever. We fall into tunnel vision, and fail to see that it is temporary. We forget that it is impermanent. That this moment, like every other, is impermanent and will not last forever.

The final step is acceptance. We find our way to accept this temporary situation and let go of our need to escape it. We reassure ourselves with that same kindness, compassion, and patience, that 'it is like this now, but I am okay, and I am going to be okay'. By mustering the courage to find some level of equanimity in the face of overwhelm, we find we have confidence that the storm will pass. We choose to trust that we can weather the storm and get through it.

The aim of the practice of proactively dealing with overwhelm is to develop emotional resilience. Learning to ride out the inevitable storms of life rather than succumbing to them and being tossed about by them is a superpower that will immensely enrich our lives and reduce our suffering. Even though these experiences are uncomfortable, we remind ourselves that feelings can never harm us; they can never hurt us. And they never last forever. That's what practical dharma offers us when we feel overwhelmed.

Reflection

✦   Think of a recent situation in which you felt overwhelmed. How might the practice of noticing and acknowledging your feelings have changed your response to that situation?

IV • Actualize a path

In this section, we emphasize the importance of taking action once we have practiced and understood the first three tasks; we set an intention to meet life's challenges with a strong ethical foundation, a mindful view, and skillful responding instead of reactivity.

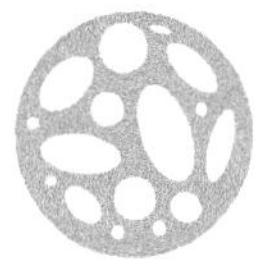

14. Ethics and appropriate living

As a bee gathering nectar does not harm or disturb the color and fragrance of the flower; so do the wise move through the world.
The Buddha

At its heart, Buddhism offers a practical framework for living a life of integrity, mindfulness, and compassion. From a secular perspective, as articulated by thinkers like Stephen Batchelor and Winton Higgins, Buddhist ethics are not based on metaphysical or religious beliefs, but rather on a shared commitment to alleviate suffering and foster human flourishing. We don't act ethically out of fear of divine retribution. This approach views Buddhist teachings as tools for navigating the challenges of everyday life, helping us align our deepest values and aspirations with our actions.

Buddhist ethics, grounded in principles like compassion, mindfulness, and wisdom, invite us to engage with life in a way that reduces harm and promotes well-being – for ourselves, for others, and for the planet. Rather than focusing on esoteric or ritualistic aspects of Buddhism, a secular approach emphasizes the practical application of ethical principles, encouraging us to reflect on the motivations and consequences of our actions in the context of modern life. We approach each ethical question without preconceived ideas, instead viewing it with discernment and wisdom.

This chapter explores how foundational ethical principles from Buddhism, such as the five precepts and elements of the eightfold path, can serve as guides for mindful, compassionate living. Not as dogmatic rules but as broad templates for addressing ethical questions. Which is to say that these principles are not rigid commandments but rather an invitation to develop greater awareness, responsibility, and kindness in our daily choices and interactions. The precepts are not inclusive of all ethical challenges yet they provide a good framework and 'jumping off' point for our important and necessary ethical journey.

The five lay precepts form the cornerstone of Buddhist ethics for non-monastics. In a secular context, these precepts are not seen as moral absolutes handed down from an external authority, but as personal commitments to live by in a way that minimizes harm and cultivates well-being. They are less about adhering to a set of rules and more about fostering self-awareness and intentionality in our actions. Ethics are foundational to the Buddhist path – helping us lead 'a life of rigorous ethical commitment', as Stephen Batchelor puts it.

✦   Refraining from killing or harming living beings

The first precept calls on us to avoid causing harm to others – be they humans, other beings, or the environment. This principle is rooted in care and compassion, and an awareness of the interconnectedness of all life. From a secular perspective, this precept encourages us to reflect on the impact of our actions, whether it's the food we consume, the way we handle conflict, or how we engage with the natural world.

In practical terms, this could mean adopting habits like eating less or no meat, supporting sustainable practices, or resolving disputes with patience and empathy. It is about cultivating a mindset that seeks to reduce suffering wherever possible, recognizing that every choice we make carries consequences beyond ourselves.

✦ Refraining from taking what is not freely given

This precept focuses on honesty and fairness. It invites us to avoid stealing, exploiting others, or taking more than our fair share. In a broader sense, it also encourages us to reflect on how our actions contribute to systems of inequality or harm.

Living by this precept might involve practicing gratitude for what we have, being mindful of how we use resources, and fostering generosity. In a consumer-driven and acquisitive world driven by greed, it challenges us to question habits of overconsumption and entitlement, helping us cultivate a sense of sufficiency and a spirit of giving.

✦ Refraining from sexual misconduct

This third precept is about fostering respect, trust, and care in our relationships. It calls on us to approach intimacy with mindfulness, consent, and integrity, avoiding actions that exploit or harm others.

From a secular perspective, this encourages us to reflect on the dynamics of power, attachment, and desire in our personal relationships. It challenges us to be honest with ourselves and others, to honor commitments, and to approach sexuality in ways that are ethical, non-harming, and supportive of mutual well-being.

✦ Refraining from false speech

The fourth precept highlights the profound impact of our words. It encourages us to avoid lying, gossiping, or using language to manipulate or harm, and instead to speak in ways that foster understanding, kindness, and trust.

In today's interconnected world, this precept has particular relevance for how we communicate online. It invites us to pause before we speak or post, asking whether our words are true, necessary, and constructive. Practicing mindful communication helps us build deeper connections and reduce harm in our interactions.

✦ Refraining from intoxicants that cloud the mind

The fifth precept is about maintaining clarity and mindfulness by avoiding substances or habits that impair our judgment or awareness. While traditionally referring to alcohol and drugs, this precept can also be understood more broadly as a call to examine habits such as escapism, distraction, and overindulgence.

From a secular perspective, this precept encourages us to live with intention and balance. Whether it's reducing screen time, moderating consumption, or cultivating healthier habits, the goal is to support a clear and focused mind that can respond to life with wisdom and care.

A key feature of Buddhist ethics is its emphasis on intention. Unlike rule-based systems that focus solely on external actions, Buddhist ethics prioritize the motivations behind our behavior. For example, an act of generosity performed out of genuine care carries more ethical weight than the same act done for recognition or self-interest.

From a secular standpoint, this focus on intention invites us to cultivate qualities like compassion, empathy, and mindfulness. By paying close attention to the reasons we act, we can ensure that our choices align with our values and contribute to the well-being of others.

The ethical dimension of the noble eightfold path provides further guidance for living with integrity. In particular, the principles of appropriate speech, appropriate action, and appropriate livelihood offer practical tools for aligning our actions with our values.

Appropriate speech emphasizes the importance of using language to build trust and understanding. It encourages us to avoid lying, divisive speech, and harmful words, and instead to communicate with honesty, kindness, and purpose.

In practice, this might involve mindful listening, pausing before speaking, or choosing words that promote connection rather than conflict. In the digital age, it also means being intentional about how we engage on social media, ensuring that our interactions reflect our ethical commitments.

Appropriate action focuses on living in ways that promote safety, fairness, and well-being. It calls on us to refrain from harm, theft, and misconduct, and to act in ways that contribute to the common good.

This might involve making small, thoughtful choices – such as supporting ethical businesses, reducing waste, or advocating for social justice. By aligning our actions with our values, we can contribute to a more compassionate and equitable world.

Appropriate livelihood highlights the importance of earning a living in ways that are ethical and do not cause harm. This includes avoiding professions that exploit others, non-human species, or the environment, and seeking work that contributes to human and ecological well-being. In today's context, this might mean advocating for workplace ethics, supporting fair trade practices, or finding ways to align our careers with our broader purpose and values.

Mindfulness is central to the practice of Buddhist ethics. By cultivating present-moment awareness, we develop the ability to observe our thoughts, emotions, and actions without judgment. This awareness helps us respond to situations with clarity and intention rather than reacting impulsively.

Deepening our understanding of interconnectedness allows us to recognize the impact of our actions on others and the world. By practicing present moment awareness, we can approach ethical living with greater wisdom and compassion, making choices that align with our deepest values.

A secular approach to Buddhist ethics emphasizes their relevance to modern life and their potential to create a more compassionate, just, and sustainable world. Ethical living is not about perfection or rigid adherence to rules; it is a dynamic process of reflection, growth, and engagement.

By living with mindfulness, compassion, and intention, we can reduce harm, foster meaningful connections, and contribute to the well-being of all and human flourishing by supporting projects such as a better health system for all, and the replacement of burning fossil fuels with sustainably produced electricity. In doing so, we embody the timeless wisdom of the Buddha in a way that resonates with the challenges and complexities of the 21st century. This is the essence of secular Buddhist ethics: a practical path toward greater harmony, understanding, and human flourishing.

Reflection

✦ How can guidelines such as the five precepts serve as guideposts in your daily life rather than rigid moral rules? What role does intention play in ethical decision-making?

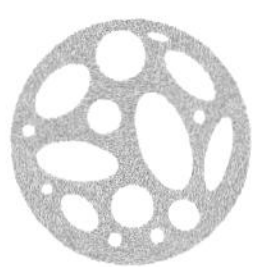

15. Mindfulness and meditation practice

Mindfulness is about being fully awake in our lives. It is about perceiving the exquisite vividness of each moment. We also gain immediate access to our own powerful inner resources for insight, transformation, and healing.

Jon Kabat-Zinn

Mindfulness has become embedded in our culture in the recent past. A simple Google search makes the point. It is everywhere on YouTube and there are hundreds of podcasts on mindfulness as well as multiple mindfulness apps for smartphones.

Mindfulness has been monetized in a way the Buddha could not have imagined. Some are making millions of dollars selling mindfulness. It is on the cover of every magazine in the checkout line at the supermarket. Every organization, small to large, has incorporated it into its human resources offerings as part of our therapeutic culture. It is offered as a cure for everything from anxiety to insomnia to a myriad of physical ills.

Meditation has been separated from its Buddhist roots in the move to popularize mindfulness practice. This separation is not without cost. Without a foundation in situational ethics and wisdom, mindfulness practice is just another self-improvement technique directed at those who are anxious, those functioning below their potential on the job, and those seeking stress reduction. The practical benefits of this secular mindfulness meditation are touted as lowering stress, decreasing depression, improving memory, and strengthening relationships. While these goals are not without their usefulness, they are a limited use of this ancient practice.

Appropriate mindfulness is the seventh of the eight components of the eightfold path and an essential part of the path that the Buddha taught. Though it can be a challenging practice, especially for beginners, it is cultivating awareness of oneself, one's feelings, thoughts, and the nature of reality. The full benefit of mindfulness comes from paying attention to sensations, feelings, thoughts, and surroundings in the moment from a position of non-judgment and acceptance.

For those new to meditation, this may sound mysterious and abstract. In practice, the instructions are relatively straightforward. The benefits may not be readily apparent so it is important to give the practice at least two to three months before rendering a verdict on your practice of meditation.

With mindfulness comes the ability to deal with the feelings and movements of the mind peacefully with detachment and wise understanding. This may sound complex and challenging because mindfulness practice is experiential and not easily described in words. It is not simply the practice of bare attention that the Buddha described though that is one ingredient. The Buddha did not give specific instructions on how to practice mindfulness. Rather, he taught that there are four aspects of mindfulness we need to include in our practice. They are:

✦　Mindfulness of the body

This includes mindfulness of breathing, posture, comprehension, bodily functions, material elements such as earth, wind, fire, and water, and the impermanence of the body.

✦　Mindfulness of feelings

This second aspect includes attention to feeling tones, not emotions. Is our immediate experience pleasant? Unpleasant? Neutral?

✦　Mindfulness of mind states

The focus here is on our state of mind. Does it contain greed, hatred, and delusion, or is it free of these states? Is it distracted? Developed or undeveloped? Concentrated or scattered? Free or bound?

✦　Mindfulness of the dharmas

This category is esoteric and beyond the scope of this book, other than to say it includes mindfulness of the five hindrances which are barriers to our meditation practice. The five hindrances are sensual desire, ill will, restlessness and worry, doubt, and sloth and torpor. Mindfulness of the dharmas also includes mindfulness of the four tasks.

The four foundations of mindfulness that the Buddha taught cover virtually all of our experience, including our mental experience which is covered by the fourth category. He asks us to be fully present with all experience as we cultivate new levels of self-awareness. Doing so is the key to freeing us from the grasping and clinging in all areas of our life which causes so much suffering. We set the intention to cultivate clarity about the fullness of our experience.

Mindfulness is an active process; it is not 'spacing out' on life or achieving altered states of consciousness. One of the goals of meditation is to cultivate non-judgmental awareness of the totality of our experience; we are not living our lives on autopilot. Instead, we feel connected to our experience. We are not pushing it away if it is unpleasant or clinging to it if it is pleasant. We bring an open-minded curiosity to our experiences as we watch them arise.

Before establishing a regular meditation practice, I lived my life largely on autopilot. Day after day, I functioned mindlessly much of the time, lost in unproductive thought about meaningless topics. Every day seemed like the previous one, regularly interrupted by some manifestation of my suffering or self-judgment. I was bored and unhappy, and my life lacked joy or richness. Each day was predictable and days flew by with a notable sameness. I took things for granted without appreciating the bounty of life.

Starting a mindfulness practice woke me up to the pattern into which my life had fallen. I began to pay attention to my surroundings and my choices became clearer and consistent with how I wanted to live my life. I was no longer the passenger; I was the driver. Boredom decreased and more joy began to come into my daily life as I appreciated all the gifts of life. I no longer took so much for granted. Brought together with the teachings of the dharma, daily life started making sense to me, and have meaning.

Meditation practice helps us develop greater discernment regarding our experiences, and wisdom about life as it is, not as we wish it to be. Meditation practice is not a means of ridding ourselves of those aspects of our behavior or personality that we dislike. Instead, it is a means of changing the relationship with aspects of who we are. We become less judgmental about ourselves and are more inclined to accept all parts of ourselves with compassion. We begin to see that perfection is not achievable, and begin to give up the quest for it.

If you are not currently a meditator, I suggest that meditation is best learned in real time with guidance from a teacher. I recommend that you join a meditation group, take a class, or avail yourself of guided instructions on the Internet. If you want to begin on your own, you will find a brief instruction below.

The instructions are straightforward and relatively brief. However, the practice requires discipline and a willingness to set aside time daily. Remember that this is an active, engaged, and purposeful activity – not a time to make a grocery list. Your mind will constantly wander, because this is what our minds do. Our task is to return to our anchor point, typically the breath, each time we realize that the mind has wandered. And we always do so with kindness and without judgment.

Find a comfortable sitting posture that is upright and alert in a quiet room.

It is best not to have your back supported as you may fall asleep once you begin to relax.

Set a timer for 5 to 10 minutes if you have never meditated.

Take a couple of slow deep breaths with your eyes closed.

Let your breath settle into a natural rhythm.

Do not try to control the breath.

Rest your attention on the breath at the tip of the nostril as it enters or leaves the nose.

Pay attention to the mind as it wanders into thoughts.

This is normal and will happen frequently.

When you notice that it has happened, very gently, without judgment, return an awareness of the breath.

Continue this practice until the time is up and slowly open your eyes.

Take a moment to come back into outward-directed attention.

Set aside time each day for this practice.

Gradually increase the length of time for your daily meditation until you reach 30 to 45 minutes.

For mindfulness to be other than a means of stress reduction, it requires a solid ethical foundation. All the world's faith traditions, Buddhism included, have such a foundation. The central question is whether we can ever be truly happy if the way we live is contrary to our core values and ethics. This is why we look to the Buddha's teachings for guideposts on living an ethical life that is consistent with our values. The eightfold path provides a game plan for living ethically in concert with our meditation practice.

An instruction as simple as 'do no harm' provides guidance on living an ethical life. No such instruction is regularly offered in commercial mindfulness. I am not suggesting that anything goes with commercial mindfulness. Instead of being explicit about an ethical foundation, any such foundation in commercial mindfulness is rarely apparent. While those in medicine, and the helping professions who use mindfulness in their practices typically adhere to their professional codes of ethical conduct, their ethics are not necessarily accessible to those to whom they prescribe mindfulness.

Mindfulness alone is not an antidote for immoral or unethical behavior. It requires the underlying wisdom and guidance that the Buddha offered and the application of discernment and wisdom in response to the ethical dilemmas that we encounter.

One of the appeals of secular Buddhism to me is that it does not deal in absolutes or rigid rules, as other faith traditions do. It gives us guideposts with which to mindfully contemplate a course of action that is ethical and does no harm. The responsibility for making wise ethical choices falls squarely in our laps. We are not threatened with eternal damnation or other punishments should we fall short in our efforts.

Buddhism is not a judging or shaming tradition. It is loving and compassionate. It accepts our human frailties. As we cultivate these qualities, our ethical foundation is strengthened because we care for ourselves and others. We want to do right. Our participation in a community such as a sangha further supports our ethical behavior. What the Buddha taught was not based on faith or metaphysical beliefs or requirements. Instead, he asks us to take individual responsibility for following his teachings and living a life informed by our values. We are guided by the wisdom achieved through our regular meditation practice and our honest discernment of ethical questions in concert with the ancient teachings of the Buddha.

Reflection

✦ Have you tried to meditate and had no success? Are you willing to try again, possibly with the help of a group or teacher?

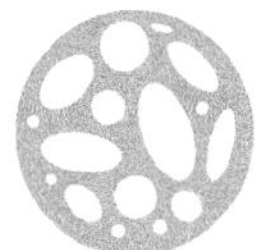

16. Integrating the path

The dharma is the most precious thing in the world and we should put it at the center of our hearts and transform our whole lives into dharma practice. Otherwise, at the time of death, we will look back and say, now what was all that about? If we truly want to benefit others and ourselves, we have to do it. No excuses.
Tenzin Palmo

The Buddha's teachings, at their core, aim to liberate us from suffering and guide us toward a life of peace, clarity, and fulfillment. Our intention is to focus on Gotama's most fundamental and practical teachings – which are not meant to be abstract or esoteric, but a path to be lived and practiced in our day-to-day lives. While Buddhist philosophy is vast and multifaceted, its ultimate goal is profoundly simple: to help us understand the nature of suffering, how it arises, and how it can be overcome. In so doing, it invites us to live with greater awareness, compassion, and freedom.

The practices offered by secular dharma provide the transformative power of integrating the dharma into daily life. By combining Gotama's teachings with evidence-based psychology an approach is offered that bridges ancient wisdom with modern science, making it accessible and relevant to our modern times. The Buddha's teachings – and their practical application – offer a path out of this cycle of suffering, not by escaping life's difficulties but by meeting them with mindfulness, acceptance, and compassion.

What makes these teachings so powerful is their practicality. They are not abstract doctrines to be admired from a distance but tools to be used in the messy, complicated realities of everyday life. For instance, mindfulness enables us to be present with our experiences as they unfold, without judgment or resistance. Whether we are facing a difficult conversation, a moment of joy, or the pain of loss, mindfulness allows us to meet each moment with clarity and openness. This simple shift in perspective can profoundly change the way we relate to our lives, helping us to reduce stress, make wiser choices, and cultivate a sense of inner peace.

Over the years my decision to combine the Buddha's teachings with evidence-based psychology highlighted an important truth: the principles of the dharma are not confined to any one culture or time period. Modern psychology, with its focus on understanding the mind and improving well-being, often parallels Buddhist teachings. Many modern psychology treatment protocols draw heavily from Buddhist concepts, particularly the idea that our thoughts and reactions play a significant role in shaping our experiences. Just as the Buddha taught that we can change the way we relate to suffering by examining and transforming our mental habits, modern psychology affirms that we can rewire our thought patterns to reduce distress and enhance well-being. This integration makes the dharma more relevant to those who might otherwise find it intimidating or overly philosophical, demonstrating that its teachings are not only accessible but also scientifically validated.

My personal transformation is a testament to the power of the dharma when applied with sincerity and commitment. Gotama often emphasized that his teachings are not meant to be taken on faith alone but to be tested and experienced directly. This experiential approach is what makes the dharma so transformative. By practicing mindfulness, ethical living, and compassionate action, we begin to see changes not only in our inner world but also in our relationships, our work, and overall sense of purpose.

This transformation does not mean that life becomes free of challenges. As we all know, life is hard, and suffering is inevitable. The dharma does not promise to eliminate all difficulties. It does, however, offer us tools to navigate them with wisdom and grace. When we approach life with acceptance – embracing its joys and sorrows without clinging or aversion – we free ourselves from much of the unnecessary suffering that arises from resistance and attachment. This acceptance is not passive resignation but a courageous willingness to face reality as it is, moment by moment.

The idea that 'we need not remain prisoners of our past' is central to both evidence-based psychology and the Buddhist path. While our past experiences and conditioning shape us, they do not define us. Through mindfulness and self-awareness, we can begin to see the habits of the mind that keep us stuck so that we can make conscious choices to move in a different direction. This sense of agency is both empowering and liberating, reminding us that change is always possible, no matter how entrenched our habits may seem.

Ultimately, the goal of the dharma is to help us live a more awakened life. This does not mean achieving some lofty state of enlightenment that feels out of reach for ordinary people. Rather, it means living with greater awareness, compassion, and integrity in our daily lives. It means showing up fully for ourselves and others, making choices that align with our values, and cultivating a sense of gratitude and joy in the face of life's challenges.

My gratitude for the teachings and their impact on every aspect of my life is immeasurable and serves as a powerful reminder of what is possible when we commit to the path. By prioritizing the practices that reduce suffering and promote well-being, we not only transform our own lives but also contribute to the well-being of those around us. Gotama taught that the way we live matters – not just for ourselves but for the entire web of interconnected beings to which we belong. `

The dharma is not an exclusive practice limited to full-time monastics or spiritual elites but a universal teaching available to anyone willing to explore it. Gotama himself encouraged his followers to 'come and see' for themselves, to test the teachings in their own lives and see what works. This spirit of openness and experimentation is at the heart of the dharma.

My hope is that you find the themes of this book – a focus on practical teachings, the integration of modern psychology, and the transformative potential of the dharma, to be a powerful guide for you to seek living with less suffering and more joy. By stepping fully into the reality of life, accepting it as it is, and choosing to cultivate mindfulness, compassion, and ethical living, we can begin to experience the freedom and fulfillment that the Buddha promised. Every day truly can feel like a gift, and by embracing the dharma, we open ourselves to the possibility of living with greater gratitude, purpose, and connection. This is the true path of awakening, and it is available to us all.

Reflection

◆ Where in your life do you want to apply the methods of practical dharma to improve the quality of your life and reduce your suffering? If you are reluctant, what is holding you back?

V • Human flourishing

In this section we see that what Gotama taught was not about achieving mystical experiences, but rather how to live a fully engaged, flourishing life; this flourishing is available to all of us if we avail ourselves of the Buddha's wisdom.

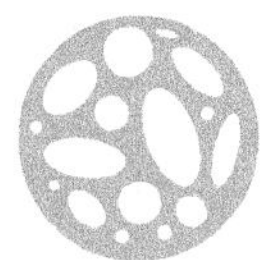

17. Gratitude and contentment

These two people are hard to find in the world. Which two? The one who is first to do a kindness, and the one who is grateful and thankful for a kindness done.

The Buddha

When I was a child, my mother always said, 'count your blessings' whenever I whined or complained. It felt like a guilt trip, so her admonition had no resonance with me. Who would have imagined that her words would return to me as an adult and strongly inform my embrace of the dharma?

Practical dharma applied in our day-to-day lives reduces our suffering and the suffering of those around us. How can we not be grateful? Gratitude practice is one of the simplest and most powerful dharma practices that we can do to increase our happiness and reduce our suffering. We do not have to look far to practice gratitude and not just for the big things in our life. But also, the small everyday simple blessings and beauty in our lives – the wonder in our lives. This is one of my favorite and most regular practices, and it pays significant dividends in the form of greater joy and contentment.

We are surrounded by the wonder, magic, and mystery of life and all creation. We only need to wake up and experience gratitude for the world in which we live. This means taking nothing for granted which, unfortunately, is something we do every day in our busy lives. The practice is as simple as engaging in the mindful cultivation of gratitude daily.

I begin each day with a gratitude practice for the many blessings in my life. As best I can, I presume nothing. I now view every day as a gift as are all the details of my life. The practice has profoundly increased my happiness and reduced my suffering.

Gratitude balances the mind's tendency to focus on the negative and on what we feel is lacking in our life. The practice frees us from our usual litany of dissatisfactions. We have greater clarity of thinking and feel more connected to life. Mental spaciousness occurs and self-centered ego concerns lessen in importance.

I always start with gratitude for the human birth of which I am the product. The gift of this singular life – a miracle in the vastness of time and space that randomly joined sperm and ovum to create a life. How can I not express gratitude for such a miracle?

Gratitude practice helps us see that everything is interconnected and that none of us can survive independently. We depend on the natural world and thousands of other humans to meet our daily needs for food, shelter, protection, information, and safety. We think about the abundance in our lives and acknowledge the individual acts of others that produced such bounty. As written in the Hebrew Bible, 'we all drink from wells we did not dig and are warmed by fires we did not build'.

For example, when I read my morning newspaper, I think about the reporter who gathered the news, the person who felled the tree to make the paper it is printed on, the truck driver who took the logs to the paper factory, the people in the factory who turned the wood pulp into newsprint, those who manufactured the ink with which the paper is printed, the typesetter who for-matted the pages, the printer who printed my copy, the distributor who brought the papers to my city, and the delivery person who delivered it to my front door every morning, rain or shine. With a feeling of deep gratitude, I bow to them all.

Our hearts open when we practice gratitude. Feelings of generosity – of wanting to express our gratitude by practicing generosity arise. Gratitude practice does not mean that we deny life's difficulties. We fully recognize and embrace our challenges and suffering. However, gratitude practice prepares us to face problems with greater equanimity and resilience.

Can we even be grateful even for the challenges in our life? Seeing obstacles as teachers can help us use the gifts of the Buddha's wisdom to create spaciousness and perspective in our lives. We welcome every experience as a potential teacher.

A benefit of gratitude practice is discovering wonder and awe about the world. We see the world with new eyes in what Zen calls 'beginner's mind'. We see the forest and the trees as well as all the living creatures therein. We stand in awe of the vast complexity of the world and the universe surrounding us.

Gratitude also derives from an appreciation for seeing that we learn from setbacks. Toxic emotions like anger, irritation, self-ishness, envy, and greed are neutralized. Wonder, awe, and gratitude are antidotes to feelings of loss, deprivation, scarcity, despair, and hopelessness. Our heart is full and open and joy happens. The Chinese proverb, 'one joy scatters a hundred griefs' sums it up nicely.

Gratitude need not feel like an obligation. Rather, it is an appreciation for all the gifts this life provides. It is taking nothing for granted, though not in the sense of owing a debt of gratitude. Instead, it is a deeply felt appreciation that evokes feelings of generosity, its close cousin. We want to be as generous to the world as it has been to us. Nor is it an attitude of giving up, resignation, or despair like 'my life is terrible but I guess I should be grateful for what I do have'.

Gratitude brings us ultimately into the present moment. We are thankful for things that are right here right now because they are precious and impermanent. We appreciate them because we know they will not last. Gratitude practice costs us nothing but time and effort, yet the rewards are priceless.

Reflection

✦ Do you tend to focus on what is missing from your life? Or on all the gifts in your life? Consider beginning each day by bringing to mind five things for which you are grateful. Does doing so bring you more happiness and appreciation for your life?

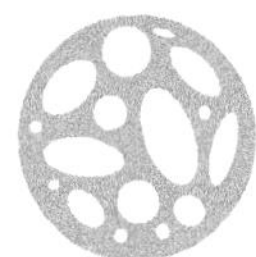

18. Wise hope and faith

Hope is being able to see that there is light despite all the darkness.
Desmond Tutu

Fyodor Dostoevsky wrote that 'to live without hope is to cease to live'. Hope truly is integral to our aliveness – but the type of hope we hold is very important.

There is an important distinction between the Buddhist view of hope and the ordinary, generic way we typically talk about hope. In Buddhism, we see so-called ordinary hope as based on desire and clinging. It contains a wanting or wishing for an outcome different from what might happen. For instance, 'I hope that it won't rain tomorrow'. Well, it's very possible that it is going to rain, and if I am attached to the idea that it should not rain, I am going to be unhappy – and for what purpose? With this application of ordinary hope, there is a fear that our wishes will not be fulfilled, the fear that we will be disappointed, and so, just as often as not, this form of hope becomes a form of suffering, and is always an expression of attachment and clinging.

While such examples of ordinary hope typically lead to suffering, wise hope is critical to our individual and collective survival and well-being. Wise hope is an attitude of the heart and mind, and is, as Dostoevsky described, essential in this human life. Wise hope helps get us out of bed in the morning, because the belief that things can and will be alright or improve is what gets us through hard times. Dostoevsky's words remind us that apathy is not an enlightened path. On the enlightened path, we are called to live with hope and possibility, knowing full well that impermanence is a central tenet of our existence.

Wise hope has no blinders. It includes seeing things as they truly are, including the truth of suffering. The eye that looks out with wise hope sees both the truth of the existence of suffering and our capacity to transform it. We aspire to accomplish certain things whilst recognizing and accepting the reality that what we are hoping for, what we are working towards, may or may not happen. With this approach, we consider the full range of true possibilities, and do not become overly attached to outcomes.

When we recognize and accept that we do not know what will happen, we keep this kind of hope alive. This is wise hope. Wise hope helps us have faith that the teachings of the Buddha will indeed reduce our suffering, without our attaching to it happening through a specific set of outcomes. In other words, rather than hope for certainty that if I only do X, then my life will be better, I cultivate a 'don't know mind'. This creates a much more spacious perspective in which I am open to a wide spectrum of possibilities as to how my suffering will lessen, even if I cannot know exactly what or when or how it will happen. I trust with wise hope that if I practice the Buddha's teachings, the rest will be revealed.

Too often we use hope and expectation interchangeably. They are not the same. Expectation focuses on specific outcomes – it is akin to our definition of ordinary hope. Wise hope is broader. It's an active, realistic outlook; a spacious perspective that is necessarily tied to, and therefore accepting of, uncertainty because we have no way of predicting or controlling the future. It is spacious because, understanding impermanence, we know that change is inevitable. Wise hope is not specific; it is more of an outlook or an attitude. A positive belief that, overall, life is a beautiful thing that's worth living, even though there is difficulty, hardship, injustice, and so on, as opposed to wishful thinking or childlike self-delusion, in which we attempt to convince ourselves and others that everything is going to work out just so because we cannot entertain the possibility that it won't.

Hoping for a specific outcome and attaching our happiness to it is an invitation for suffering. So, we need to become aware when it's happening – when our attachment to an outcome is posing as hope. We must use discernment to distinguish between hope that clings to an expectation and hope that is spacious and life-affirming.

There were periods in my life which I characterize as having a real sense of hopelessness. I saw specific outcomes as a way out. 'If only I had a new boss, my life would improve. If only I had this, that, or the other thing, all would be well again'. But such ordinary hope, which is ultimately attachment to a specific outcome, was a trap because if that very narrow and specific outcome did not happen, my suffering only worsened.

This is why we need to seek a more spacious and wise hope, because it allows for the fact that we cannot predict or control outcomes and, even so, our suffering is impermanent, and therefore things can and may improve. Patience is required – patience, and more spacious and wise hope.

Thankfully, I have had wonderful teachers who helped me see and understand this as a younger man, so my circumstances eventually changed for the better. Previously, I had spent years looking for quick fixes to my unhappiness. I hoped that the next magic bullet – typically in the form of acquiring this, learning that, or buying whatever – would bring me out of my doldrums. Each time, after the novelty of the most recent attempt wore off, I was back to being unhappy and dissatisfied. While on an extended retreat, my teacher at the time suggested that I 'give up all hope that a particular accomplishment or acquisition was the way out of my suffering'. Instead, she suggested that I should 'drop the rope of trying to fix myself' and relax into my daily meditation practice and study of the dharma.

This was a wake-up call. It instilled in me the confidence I needed to trust that cultivating wise, open, spacious hope would ultimately reduce my suffering, even if I had to accept that I had no control (which, after all, was true whether I accepted it or not). Once I began to disentangle my ego's preferences from its go-to of trying to fix myself with external changes, I relaxed and my suffering began to lessen.

In her book *Faith*, Sharon Salzberg discusses what she calls confirmed faith – that is, faith based on knowledge, not a hunch. Thanks to my experience, I have the knowledge that the dharma makes good on the promises of Gotama's teachings, which are in and of themselves broad and overarching. Faith is not just about religious adherence to dogma, which is how it is typically spoken of in our culture. Instead, faith means trust – trust that this path is worthwhile even when we're experiencing doubt.

Faith can be inspiring. It is the source of the inspiration we need to tackle the challenges and barriers we are facing in our lives. Faith can also mean confidence, as when we call on our past experiences to motivate us to meet difficulties, knowing that we have overcome them in the past. 'Hey, I've been here before. Let me ride this out. Let me bring all the best skills I can, and remember that this too shall pass.'

We cannot have wise hope without the type of faith that Salzberg describes. And when it comes to our path, faith is about trusting that the truth of the Buddha's teachings can be relied upon to lessen our suffering. Faith in these teachings has survived for 2400 years, largely because the teachings have worked all this time – for well over two millennia.

Salzberg quotes the Buddha as having said, 'faith is the beginning of all good things'. In other words, no matter what we encounter in life, if we have faith, it enables us to pick up and try again, to trust again, to love again, to keep aspiring to experience less suffering in our lives. Even in the depths of our suffering, faith reminds us that all things change, and that we can, and must, keep moving forward. I often say to myself and to others when they are suffering, 'This is impermanent – it will not last'. This belief is deeply rooted in my experience as well as in faith.

The opposite of faith is doubt. Doubt is one of the five hindrances (the barriers to mindfulness and meditation practice), along with sensual desire, ill will, restlessness and worry, and sloth and torpor. Doubt not only undermines mindfulness.' It also undermines hope.

Our challenge is to mindfully pay attention when doubt in its many forms, creeps into our practice. We may doubt the teachings. We may doubt if our practice is working. We may doubt our teachers, or the experiences we are having. We may doubt our abilities, or doubt the outcome we've been working so hard to achieve. Doubt often arises in the form of very convincing stories we tell about ourselves and our hopes and dreams. 'Oh, I'll never get this. This will never work out for me.' Doubt is a dangerous hindrance because it so often goes unnoticed. It can pull us away from our practice. It can discourage us and make us want to throw in the towel. It can cause us to lose hope, and our connection to faith.

This is why it's so important to cultivate faith, and to create the opportunity to experience confirmed faith, as characterized by Sharon Salzberg, by staying with our practice especially in challenging times, and by reflecting on the benefits of the practice we have witnessed in ourselves or others.

Faith in Buddhist practice is not blind adherence to dogma or a belief in the supernatural. Rather, it is a deeply rooted trust in the transformative potential of the path, and the efficacy of the teachings. It is the willingness to begin and to stay with the practice, despite uncertainty, doubt, or difficulty. It is an invitation to explore the teachings experientially, to see for ourselves whether they lead to greater freedom, wisdom, and compassion. This quality of faith becomes especially crucial in times of challenge, when our resolve may waiver, and the mind is more prone to discouragement or distraction.

Faith and practice are deeply interconnected. Faith inspires us to practice, and practice, in turn, deepens our faith. This cyclical relationship sustains us through the inevitable ups and downs of life. Just as a seed cannot grow without sunlight and water, our spiritual growth relies on the nourishment of trust – trust in the teachings, trust in the practice, and trust in our potential to awaken. At its core, faith in Buddhism is not about believing in something external, but about believing in our own capacity to experience moments of awakening, and the efficacy of the tools we are using to do so.

I want to close with a Japanese proverb. 'Fall seven times, stand up eight'. This is an application of wise and resilient hope.

Reflection

✦ How can you distinguish between ordinary hope and wise hope in your personal experiences? Reflect on a time when faith played a crucial role in overcoming a challenge in your life. How did faith influence your perspective and actions during this period? How did it support the outcome?

VI • RELATIONSHIPS

In this section we look at the centrality of relationships in our lives. How our relationships are informed by every aspect of the dharma resulting in both great joy and great suffering; as I tell my students, 'relationships are where the rubber meets the road on our path'.

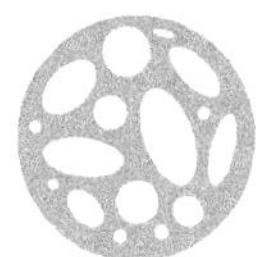

19. Relationships: connection and impermanence

A family is a place where minds come in contact with one another.
If these minds love one another, the home will be as beautiful as
a flower garden. But if these minds get out of harmony with one
another, it is like a storm that plays havoc with the garden.
  Bukkyo Dendo Kyokai

We are relational beings. Our ancient ancestors' very survival depended on their cooperative relationships in a tribe or community. However, we all find that our unskillful feelings and behaviors show up in our relationships which makes them one of the most challenging areas of our practice. The tools of the dharma offer multiple options for addressing the pitfalls we encounter in our relationships.

Human beings evolved to live in family and tribal groupings, and this is how we survived as a species. To be cast out of or shunned by others in one's tribe or group is one of the most painful experiences humans can have. Two hundred thousand years ago it meant certain death on the savannahs of Africa. Simply put, our ancestors either learned to get along or they would die. Yet we are still trying to figure out how to get along. Practical dharma offers some answers.

Relationships are central to the human experience. We need them for survival, community, connection, intimacy, procreation, cooperation, and safety. These relationships are with our parents, siblings, mates, children, friends, bosses, and co-workers, and anyone with whom we have interactions. We have many relationships, each with varying degrees of intimacy, from the closest to the most casual. It is an axiom in my profession that the more intimate the relationship, the more likely we are to get tripped up and behave or speak unskillfully.

Relationships are primarily where we get conflicted, triggered, challenged, humbled, hurt, and angry; they have the potential to cause great suffering. They are where we reenact patterns from significant early attachments where we bring all our old hurts and wounds, expectations, and longings, often unconsciously.

Relationships are also where we experience exhilaration, validation, joy, closeness, safety, comfort, and a sense of belonging, of being seen, heard, and validated. They are indeed one of the greatest joys of being human.

Before addressing specific relationship challenges let me remind you that our relationships, in all of their complexity, are no less subject to the experience of impermanence than any other phenomenon. Not only in the sense that they eventually end, whether through leaving, divorce, or death, but that they are ever-changing and not fixed from moment to moment, day-to-day, and year-to-year. It is essential that we do not cling to a fixed notion of the nature of our primary relationships; if we do, suffering is guaranteed. Instead, we must attempt to accept the ever-changing and ever-evolving nature of our relationships. The so-called honeymoon phase of a new, exciting, committed relationship with a partner bears little resemblance to the day-to-day relationship of many years.

To understand relationship challenges we must look at the primary areas from both a dharmic and relational perspective that present the most challenges as we seek loving, intimate, and functional relationships. These factors are not separate or discrete but are interwoven and overlapping. You will recognize some familiar themes:

✦ Ego

The fixed belief in a permanent solid self is a key source of suffering according to Gotama. Many, if not most, problematic relationship issues are born of ego needs. These include competition and winning, self-importance and narcissism, moral superiority, privilege, selfishness, and entitlement among others. Driven by our ego we want to win every argument, have the last word, and be the alpha. All these issues are toxic to the goal of positive relationships as they are antithetical to compassion, empathy, and deep emotional connection. Conflict, anger, resentment, withdrawal, contempt, and other unskillful responses may result.

✦ Absence of presence

This refers to 'not showing up' for the other person, and includes not fully listening, not trying to understand, and not 'walking in their shoes'. Absence of presence also includes judging, criticizing, dismissing, mocking, lacking understanding, and not offering our full and undivided attention when required – not being present for the difficulties and challenges that arise. Instead, we withdraw or push the other person away. Too often we are unwilling to stick around for the hard part of a relationship which requires a great deal of work. Do not think otherwise. We cannot just go through the motions. We need to show up by being fully engaged with significant others, including deep listening, compassion, empathy, and kindness. True intimacy deepens our connection to others which provides security and safety and lessens our suffering. It provides a refuge from the challenges of life. It is one of the true joys of being human. But we have to earn it; it is not our birthright.

✦ Relational grasping and clinging

I am intimately familiar with this one. The belief that others should act as we wish, not as they are. We have fixed expectations, outside of our conscious awareness, where we revisit old patterns of feeling rejected, not seen, not heard, misunderstood, and devalued, all of which we impose on others in our life. Attempting to control the other person is common in this situation. This is a huge source of suffering in our relationships, both intimate and casual – with our partner ('Why isn't she/he more supportive?'), with our children ('Why don't they do what I tell them?'), and even with the bank teller ('Can't they see I'm in a hurry?'). This type of relationship issue is an equal opportunity source of suffering. We suffer as does the other person. Tremendous strain is put on the relationship and withdrawal and/or avoidance by one or both parties ensue. Closeness and intimacy cease and distrust results

✦ Emotional reactivity

In relationships, reactivity is born of the prior three challenges: 1) when our ego is threatened; 2) when presence is lacking; or 3) grasping and clinging to expectations are present.

While this is not a complete list of relationship challenges, these are most often present when reactivity and relationship dysfunction occurs.

That appropriate speech prevails in our family relationships remains a formidable challenge, as that is where some of our most challenging communications occur. It is where we most often 'get our buttons pushed'. With wisdom, we enter family situations with the knowledge and expectation that lifelong patterns get triggered – forewarned is forearmed – so we can attempt to plan and implement more skillful means.

We cannot be completely free of reactivity as we are human beings and emotional creatures. Rather, we seek to manage our emotions more skillfully to reduce and attenuate them. To manage our reactivity, the underlying process with the prior relationship challenges mentioned above is to notice when something is arising, cueing us that we are uncomfortable. We are more vulnerable to reactivity when feeling insecure, alone, easily threatened, misunderstood, or marginalized. When we expect the old patterns to emerge, we unconsciously shift into a hypervigilant mode awaiting perceived relational danger, becoming guarded and distrustful. If we do not notice, there is a high likelihood of being triggered into reactivity.

Relationship dysfunction erodes trust and goodwill so, at some level, we are always on high alert. We avoid feeling vulnerable in such fraught situations, and so we become self-protective, reactive, and verbally defensive. Our reactivity energizes and emboldens us. We enter attack mode to hide our fear, emotional pain, lack of control, feeling misunderstood, vulnerable, and fear of humiliation or embarrassment. Any emotional connection is severely strained or broken.

Relationship challenges are good news/bad news situations. The bad news is that each of us acts in individually predictable ways when things do not go our way. The causes and conditions of our lives, past and present, result in our getting triggered in uniquely predictable ways. The good news is that we have agency to employ the tools of practical dharma to learn to act less predictably since our patterns are well known to us. Again, it is about noticing, pausing, and discernment.

To build more satisfying and intimate relations we bring an

open mind and mindful awareness to our conflicts and frustrations with others. We set an intention to pay attention to what is arising within both the body and the mind and then build in the sacred pause between the trigger and our response. This is perhaps some of the most challenging work we will ever do, as the ego will strongly resist in the interest of protecting itself and/or winning. The challenge is to bring mindful awareness, moment to moment, to our interactions with others as soon as we sense tension or discord.

There are four practical dharma antidotes to the problem areas we just covered. Initially, we must commit to non-judging awareness of the problem areas we bring and accept our unskillful means without self-condemnation. Understand that these are normal human challenges, the potential for which is within all of us. We resist the tendency to blame the other person for the conflict. We immediately hit a wall if we do not accept our contributions to relationship problems and instead blame the other person. Our ego wants to win, not feel small and defeated. Discernment includes accepting our role in the conflict, clearly and non-defensively, with compassion.

✦ Wise speech

This is an essential practice which is an antidote for emotional reactivity. By bringing an attitude of wanting to solve the conflict rather than win, we set an intention to pause before we speak. This pause provides a break between whatever strong emotions we are feeling and the need to speak; this helps break the chain of reactivity which becomes tit-for-tat in a relationship conflict. I am continually amazed at how quickly a conflict abates and moves into constructive speech whenever I can do this. Here again, the pause is the essential ingredient.

✦　Mindful presence

This refers to creating a container for discussion which fosters deep connection and builds trust. It invites the other person into a safe space wherein charged issues can be discussed. Full attention is required for deep listening to understand the other person. This is not a time to formulate a counter-response while pretending to listen. Mindful presence requires our willingness to set aside our agenda, especially the need to win, for the greater good of the connection. Hospice worker, Christine Longaker, says in her chapter in the anthology, *The Wisdom of Listening*, 'You must listen with your whole being, not just your ears'. That is to say listen with your body, heart, eyes, and energy – with total presence – turning toward and listening in silence to the other person without interrupting. We fill spaces of silence with compassion and/or loving-kindness, not with our counterpoint. We allow ourselves to imagine the other person's suffering. We seek to be mindfully aware of reactivity, especially in the form of defensiveness or wanting to hit back with words.

✦　Humor

No discussion of overcoming relationship challenges would be complete without addressing the importance of humor – not sarcastic humor, not mean-spirited humor, not mocking humor. Instead, good-natured, self-deprecating humor. This type of humor requires that we laugh at ourselves and our foibles. Humor breaks down barriers and helps overcome emotional obstacles. It acts as a circuit breaker. Humor encourages vulnerability. I find it most helpful in broaching difficult or charged topics. As one colleague told me, 'humor can be used to smuggle new ideas into people's hearts'. Laughing together forges connection by releasing 'feel good' neurotransmitters in the brain.

✦   Wisdom

We seek to understand the landmines in our relationships by seeing them clearly and not through rose-colored glasses or avoiding them with denial. Understanding the tripwires fosters the development of relationship wisdom. By cultivating wisdom, we learn our triggers and those of our loved ones. Out of such wisdom comes greater compassion and empathy for ourselves and others. We cultivate the ability to put ourselves in others' shoes and to see their suffering with empathy. We acknowledge and respect their point of view. We unhook from our ego's self-interest and relinquish the need to win, to be correct, and be superior, which distorts our reality and alienates the other person. Finally, we seek to interact from a position of vulnerability even though it can be very frightening. We forgo the interests of our ego in the service of greater connection and intimacy.

The work we do in our relationships is essential to our well-being. A discordant primary relationship is antithetical to happiness and creates great suffering for both parties. As so much of our practice on this path is about acceptance and letting go, never are they more needed than in our relationships.

One of the greatest of the many gifts that this practice has given me is the significant improvement in my relationships with my wife, my children, my family, and my friends. They will tell you that I am no longer the controlling, reactive, judgmental, and driven person I was twenty-five years ago. No longer is conflict always someone else's fault, nor is every interaction and decision about me. I have learned to laugh at myself and enjoy it.

We must set an intention to bring practical dharma tools to bear on our relationships to experience a reduction in suffering in ourselves and those around us. This is one of the greatest gifts that practical dharma gives us, and that we can give ourselves and our loved ones.

Rumi, the 13th-century Persian poet, wrote, 'Your path is not to seek for love, but merely to seek and find all the barriers within yourself you have built against it'. Prescient advice for finding our way through modern relationship challenges.

I would like to share a story of a primary relationship in my life with which I struggled for many years, and which caused me great suffering. My father, who died in 2008 at 89, was a second-generation German immigrant from Detroit who was the only child of a severely alcoholic mother and a largely absent salesman father. He went to Duke University and, after graduating in the middle of the second world war, immediately enlisted in the Navy. He was a naval officer in the South Pacific for the remainder of the war, commanding a landing craft at the age of 23, transporting marines to island war zones.

While in New Orleans in 1943 for training, he met my mother at a tea given by the young ladies of New Orleans for new naval officers. Sparks flew. My mother, who had one younger brother, was the only daughter of my grandparents. Her father was the scion of an old Louisiana family. They owned Linwood, a 500-acre sugar cane plantation north of Baton Rouge, where his father and grandfather had owned 100 enslaved persons before emancipation.

A prominent attorney in New Orleans, my grandfather wanted nothing to do with my father. Nor did he want my mother to have anything to do with him. He was, in my grandfather's words, 'a Yankee and not our kind of people'. But he could not say 'No' to his only daughter, so my mother rode the train with my grandmother to San Francisco six weeks later where she married my father in a civil ceremony before he deployed to the South Pacific. When he returned from the war, he had a daughter awaiting him as well as a wife, as my older sister had been born while he was away. To the best of my knowledge, my grandfather never spoke a word to my father for the rest of his life. My father never went with us on our annual trip to New Orleans to see my grandparents during Mardi Gras, as he would not have been welcome.

After the war, my father started law school at Duke, which he did not like so he left. He joined the corporate world and worked in public relations for DuPont and Dan River Mills. In 1954, when I was six years old, he resigned from his job to attend seminary to become an Episcopal priest. My mother was very unhappy; it was not what she had signed on for. She now had to clothe and feed three children – soon to be four – on a salary just one-third of what my father earned at Dan River Mills. She was no longer living in the style to which she had become accustomed.

Their marriage was not good due to cultural differences, money issues, and because they were both psychologically damaged and emotionally immature. I was my mother's favorite. This was a mixed blessing, as it meant I was an emotional extension of her, and often at odds with my siblings. With this came expectations for perfect behavior, so that I didn't bring her shame and embarrassment. She had no idea who I was as a person, and had neither the awareness nor the curiosity to find out. All that mattered was that I was perfectly behaved, well-groomed, and reflected positively on her.

My father knew nothing about how to be a father. His alcoholic mother was emotionally intrusive when she was drinking, and emotionally distant when she was sober. His father was rarely home. As a result, he was a deeply insecure and anxious man. He was driven by a need to do good, a motive that I believe contributed to his decision to go into the priesthood. Because of his poor relationship with my mother, he avoided being at home and was almost always in the community ministering to others.

He was, however, not just that person. He was also a deeply compassionate and empathic man, even if he had difficulty showing those qualities to his children. He would spend hours every week taking care of everyone in his church and others in the community. In addition to his parish duties as the only priest of a large congregation, he became involved in the civil rights movement in the '50s and '60s. He was also a vocal advocate for improved mental health services in the state. As for his children, though, it was a case of the 'cobbler's children having no shoes'.

I longed for him to be different for almost all my life. I wanted his attention and interest. I wanted him to show pride in me – to be Ward Cleaver from the *Leave It to Beaver* show or Jim Anderson from *Father Knows Best*.

Before puberty, I tried to be perfect hoping to please him by following my mother's script; it was the only one I had. But it was to no avail as he was rarely around to notice. With the onset of puberty, my hurt and rage broke through. I started acting-out, both from anger and to get his attention. Imagine his humiliation when he frequently had to pick me up at school for misbehavior or, on one occasion, at the police department for fighting. I was frequently in trouble and known as a 'troublemaker', all while living in a small town where everyone knew us.

I continued to suffer from wanting him to be different. I had fantasies of how he should be as a father, and was hurt that he did not fit my model. I desperately wanted him to take an active interest in my schoolwork, sports activities, and life, and to be a hands-on father like those on television. It was a classic case of how clinging to fixed ideas of how others should be leads to suffering. The pattern continued in different forms until he died. The experience of my relationship with him was cumulatively traumatic for me, and I know similar experiences are traumatic for many people.

As an adult I avoided him. It was too painful to be around him as I was too angry and hurt. He was anxious around me, as he felt my anger toward him and my judgment of him. He never asked about me, my work, my life, or anything. I experienced him as self-absorbed, and seethed inside whenever I had to be in his presence. When, after living in New Jersey for eleven years, I moved with my family back to Virginia in 1989, I reluctantly saw him on occasion out of obligation. It was arduous to be with him – a pattern that continued for almost twenty years until he died. We both suffered.

My father had been in assisted living due to early-onset dementia for several years before his death. He had a bad fall at the assisted living facility in early June 2008, and died in hospice two weeks later. While at the funeral home to make final arrangements (as the oldest son, I was the default person for all such tasks) the funeral director, a friend from childhood, asked if I wanted to see my father before they sent him for cremation. I declined as it seemed pointless. My wife, in her wisdom, encouraged me to do so. I reluctantly went into the back room of the funeral home where I was alone with him.

My father was lying on a gurney covered with a sheet except for his head and shoulders. I stood there for two to three minutes looking at him. He looked so serene and peaceful, something I was not used to seeing. In a moment of spontaneity, I went over and kissed him on the forehead and told him I loved him.

For reasons I did not understand then but now know are the result of my Buddhist practice, I had what can only be described as a moment of grace. I was overwhelmed with the awareness that I had spent my entire life clinging to the desire that he be someone other than who he was or was capable of being. This was an insight I had never had when he was alive, as I was too immersed in the dysfunctional emotions that caused so much suffering. I now know that I suffered greatly by clinging to the desire that he should be different – by holding him to an unachievable ideal that he be other than who he was capable of being. In that moment, I understood that his behavior toward me had not been intentional.

I realized how much I had suffered terribly for more than sixty years as a result of that clinging, and how much suffering I caused him with my anger, withdrawal, and avoidance. It felt as though fifty pounds of weight lifted off my shoulders in that moment. Several days later at his memorial service, I wept as I had never wept before. I grieved deeply both for him and for myself. I was free of the lifelong struggle and suffering that was a result of my clinging and grasping for a father that was never to be. I was free of the guilt over the suffering I had caused him from my avoidance and contempt.

All these years later, I feel the same. But the burden has never returned, nor has the anger, the hurt, or the frustration. I now have a greater understanding, empathy, and compassion for his life, his suffering, and his struggles. I have been able to recall positive interactions with him and feel proud of his work for social justice, civil rights, and mental health. I am grateful for the values that he imparted to me which informed my choice of profession.

My dharma practice gave me gifts that nothing else ever had with my father including forgiveness, acceptance, letting go, and compassion; freedom from all the unnecessary suffering I had both caused and endured. All from clinging to the fantasy of how he should have been. Such is the power and freedom given to us by these practices. I am very grateful for this.

Reflection

✦　What fixed expectations do you cling to with those to whom you are close? What is the impact on your relationship with that person?

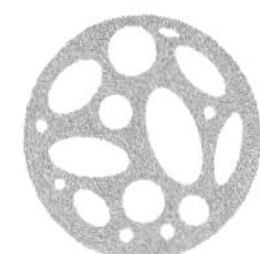

20. Healthy boundaries

'No' is a complete sentence.
Anne Lamott

In my many years of practice as a psychologist, one of the most common sources of suffering I encountered daily in my office resulted from poor interpersonal boundaries.

Interpersonal boundaries can perhaps best be described as the terms and agreements of conduct that we share between ourselves and others, as well as the personal policies we hold internally as to the treatment we will accept, and the treatment we will not accept from the people in our lives, whether it be our partner, our children, our best friend, or our boss. Boundaries are critically important to our well-being, because they are the socially applied barriers that protect us, and those with whom we interact, from being manipulated, used, disrespected, or violated. The primary purpose of setting appropriate boundaries is to ensure balance and trust in our relationships. They help us remain true to ourselves, define our needs and desires, and protect our psychological and emotional integrity. They are essential for maintaining a healthy sense of self-identity and personal space, while also fostering mutually respectful and healthy relationships.

Some of us suffer from a lack of clear or firm boundaries with others; consequently, we give away or compromise our autonomy. Other people put up walls in the form of rigid boundaries that alienate others and isolate them, leaving them alone and disconnected. Growing up with an emotionally intrusive mother who was constantly 'all up in my business', I have struggled my whole life with being able to feel safe when letting others get close to me. My rigid boundaries have loosened thanks to my dharma practice, though they still show up to this day in my relationships, typically without warning. At such times I am invited to 'practice what I preach' with practical dharma by noticing, grounding, acknowledging, and so on.

Anywhere there is a relationship between us and another person, from our most casual to our most intimate relationships, there is an interpersonal boundary – or a glaring lack of one. The style of boundary setting we have, which is typically unconscious, is the product of our early relationships with parents or caregivers and siblings. They vary from rigid protective walls at one extreme to no protective barriers at the other. Our boundary styles show up with everyone in our lives, from an intimate partner (if we have one) to people we just fleetingly encounter in the world. We may find we have one type of boundary with authority figures, another with subordinates, different ones again with an adult child, and yet another with an intimate partner.

How we establish, enforce, and honor our boundaries is a major part of who we are, and how other people experience us. As we progress on our dharma path, it is important to use discernment to understand our own individual style of setting or holding boundaries in each relational context. Failure to do so opens us up to suffering in the form of interpersonal conflict, compromising our needs and values.

Gotama taught the importance of guarding the sense doors and being mindful of our interactions. He understood well that within his sangha – as within any community – relationships can either be a source of great joy and emotional nourishment, or they can be toxic and a source of great suffering. Such is the degree of importance they carry. The outcome depends largely on how we manage the boundaries within our relationships.

Looking at the issue of boundaries through the lens of the dharma, the level of our suffering is often tied to the cultivation of (or failure to cultivate) healthy and skillful boundaries within ourselves, with others, and with all beings.

We are social beings. When our social connections are skillful, they can become foundational to our spiritual growth. When they are unskillful, they become a hindrance. Establishing clear and compassionate interpersonal boundaries is a key to walking our path with integrity. Doing so requires several important skills and behaviors including clear, open, and honest communication, respect for each person's autonomy, mutual respect of each person's values, feelings, and opinions, a sense of emotional safety, and flexibility rather than rigidity of behavior and points of view. The tools of practical dharma are invaluable in cultivating these qualities.

One of the outcomes of fuzzy, unclear, or unhealthy boundaries is burnout – an extreme state of depletion and exhaustion caused by pushing ourselves too hard for too long. This is a common problem for those of us in the helping professions who have a strong tendency towards caregiving. We spend our time and energy taking care of everyone else and, without clear boundaries, find ourselves overcommitting to the well-being of others to the extent that we compromise ourselves mentally, physically, emotionally, or all of the above. We may be unable to, or fail to, notice when our generosity has become over-giving, even though we feel emotionally or energetically depleted. Or, we might see that we are pushing past the point of well-being for someone else's sake but still feel unable to advocate for ourselves by saying, 'No, I'm actually not available to do that for you today'. In all such cases, giving, giving, and more giving (sometimes called compassion fatigue) leads to burnout.

When we have poor or porous boundaries, we leave ourselves vulnerable to taking on others' burdens at the expense of our own well-being. We become vulnerable to getting entangled in their drama, and to becoming adversely impacted by business that is not our own. This will result in losing our inner peace and equanimity in the resulting chaos, leading to resentment, burnout, and the enabling of others' unskillful behavior. And this also serves to create or worsen the suffering in our lives and, regardless of our intentions, that of the other person as well.

Conversely, rigid boundaries – those that are strictly and aggressively enforced – block the flow of attunement and compassion between us and others. Such boundaries lead to coldness and disconnection. We quickly become isolated and alone, and in a different way we accomplish the same outcome; increased suffering in our lives, and increased suffering for those who are seeking to be close to us.

The solution, as Gotama taught in relation to so many things, is to find the middle way between these two extremes – being open-hearted and compassionate, while also maintaining clear boundaries. As a wise sage said, 'we should guard ourselves as a frontier town is guarded'. This is a profound metaphor, emphasizing the importance of vigilance and self-discipline in our spiritual practice, particularly with regard to boundaries. This guarding requires constant awareness. Just as guards in a frontier town must remain vigilant at all times, we must be mindful of our thoughts, speech, and actions, ensuring they align with the principles of the eightfold path, and with all aspects of our lives, in particular our interpersonal boundaries.

In no way does this mean – nor did the Buddha ever teach – that we should be 'doormats' in our relationships. Nor should we tolerate mistreatment.

Healthy boundaries allow us to be truly compassionate with others without losing ourselves in the process. We often feel that we have to give ourselves away in order to be loved or to be compassionate. This is a misapplication. With good boundaries, we empathize with the suffering of others without taking it on as our own and thereby adding to our own suffering. We honor the emotional needs of others while honoring our own emotional needs.

Healthy boundaries allow us to offer support and kindness while assuring that others take responsibility for their own choices. A critical part of this process is knowing when to say 'yes', and when to say 'no', a process that requires discernment. We must learn to speak authentically rather than engaging in 'people-pleasing', or telling people what they want to hear. We must voice our truth when it feels necessary instead of suppressing it to keep the peace, as in, 'I'm not going to say anything because I don't want to create a conflict'. In other words, we must learn to stop 'going along just to get along'. In setting good boundaries, we honor our own autonomy in every moment and in any process. Clear boundaries protect our time and energy, which we need first and foremost for ourselves in order to live a healthy, happy life, emotionally, physically, psychologically, and spiritually.

By being skillful and intentional with our time and our boundaries, we create the inner and outer space needed for contemplation, for learning the dharma, for progress on our path, and for self-care. In addition, we are able to give our full presence in relationships because we have not overextended ourselves to the point of burnout, isolation, and resentment.

When we live with a clear sense of our own boundaries, it is easier to say 'no' to others' demands because we are better able to identify when those demands are inappropriate or excessive – or when others simply ask for more than we have available to give at that moment. We access the clarity and strength that lets us stand up for our values and commitments, even when our perspective might be unpopular or unwelcome. As social beings, this is not always easy, but it is always beneficial in the long term, both for ourselves and those with whom we are in relationship.

With practice, we develop the wisdom to know what is ours to carry and what is not, what to let in and what to let go of in our dealings with others. Healthy boundaries become like spiritual armor, rebuffing that which is challenging to our integrity while allowing in what is not – allowing us to walk the Buddhist path with courage, compassion, and grace. Ultimately, healthy boundaries help us take responsibility for our spiritual freedom, rather than giving that power away to others.

When we choose the middle way, we learn to relate skillfully without compromising our own well-being, and our relationships become a vehicle for awakening, rather than an obstacle to it. By guarding our hearts wisely with healthy boundaries, we become a clear channel for wisdom and compassion to flow through us for the benefit of all beings. In the process, we protect ourselves and navigate the world and our relationships with clarity about what is ours, and what belongs to everyone else – not rigidly, to the point of slamming the door on everyone, but with loving-kindness, deep compassion, and kind but firm limits. Balance, the middle way that the Buddha taught, is truly the secret to healthy boundaries.

Reflection

✦ Can you identify your personal style of setting boundaries in different types of relationships, and what changes might you consider for healthier interactions? In what ways can the concept of 'guarding yourself as a frontier town is guarded' be applied to your daily life to balance openness and protection?

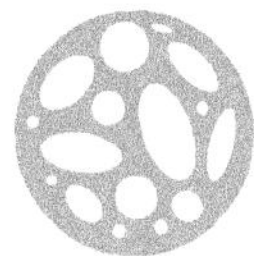

21. Acceptance and letting go

Accepting all the good and bad about someone. It's a great thing to aspire to. The hard part is actually doing it.
Sarah Dessen

One of the most consistently challenging areas in our lives is our relationships with others as I described in an earlier chapter and in the description of my relationship with my father. It doesn't matter if we are talking about the people closest to us, or people with whom we have casual encounters, the challenge is the same: accepting others as they are, not as we want them to be.

Again and again, so much suffering originates in our tendency to want people to behave in ways that we think they should. We tend to believe that if only people are more to our liking, less prone to habits and behaviors that we find annoying or challenging, how blissful our lives would be. The range of behaviors that we might believe others should change about themselves can vary from minor annoyances that may accumulate and get under our skin – leaving dishes in the sink, socks on the floor, cabinet doors open – to far more confronting behaviors like being (or feeling) corrected, judged, or even controlled.

It probably comes as no surprise to know that our ego plays a major role in such situations. Once again, when we find others behavior wanting, we are in the process of wanting things to be the way we want them to be, rather than the way that they are. Of course, we are free to ask others to change, so long as we are also able to acknowledge that we have no control over whether or not they choose to do so, since that is their choice and theirs alone to make. It is when we cling to the idea that they have to change, often silently, that everybody suffers most. We may hold this grudge against them without articulating it, for example, and in doing so cause unspoken friction in the relationship that often leads to feelings of confusion on their part, and resulting in alienation and deeper rifts of misunderstanding in the relationship. The outcome is a breakdown in honest communication that causes emotional distance, unspoken resentments and, ultimately, if left unchecked, the dissolution of the relationship. In my work with couples, the issue of accepting the other as they are and giving up efforts to have them change was a central challenge and necessity my patients faced. So much relationship dysfunction can be attributed to this issue, and my work became much more effective once I shifted the emphasis in therapy to this theme.

Of course, it's not only romantic relationships where this issue arises; it occurs between friends, co-workers, extended family members – some of us may even feel this way about the person who delivers our mail. Those of us who have known the joy and sorrow of parenting know well how difficult it is to let our children be their own people, as opposed to the people we think they could or should be. Rarely, in our culture, do parents celebrate and encourage their children's individuality, and this results in suffering for everyone.

Having been on the receiving end of such treatment as a child, it's been all the more necessary for me to observe myself as a parent wanting not to pass on such a dynamic, to the extent that I was able. I grew up feeling deeply resentful, devalued, and misunderstood because my mother constantly tried to shape me into an image that aligned with her idea of who I should be. My mother's efforts were pervasive: she sought to manage how I dressed, what my interests were, the quality of my manners and social graces, and my extracurricular activities. My personal choices and preferences were discouraged or ignored. She called me her 'little lawyer' in reference to her father, an attorney, a not-so-subtle way of conveying her wish that I should pursue such a path.

When I reached adolescence, I rebelled and began acting out in ways that ran contrary to all of her efforts to shape me. But she never relented, and on her dying day, at age 93, she was still questioning my lifestyle choices. Her failure to accept my choices and the devaluation that I felt, continue to challenge me to this day. Such is the impact of a parent trying to shape and control our behavior. Only by consciously recognizing the internalized expectations can we work to set them aside.

If we look closely enough, we'll see that the judgments we make of others, we also apply to ourselves. By the same token that we grow angry or reject others for their perceived flaws and faults, we pass the same judgments on ourselves, most often without knowing, chastising ourselves when we do not meet the same arbitrary standards we have set for others. If we are truly to accept others as they are, we must go to the source of judgment within us that finds others – and ourselves – wanting, and choose to extend that same generous acceptance to ourselves that we seek to offer to (and receive from) others.

Can we accept ourselves as we are, not as we might wish we were? This is the central question, the answer to which will reveal whether we can extend the same grace to any and every other person in our lives as well.

Once we begin to look closely – with mindfulness and discernment – at how often we get upset when others do not behave as we think they should, we begin to see it everywhere: the clerk who does not move the line along quickly enough at the grocery store; the driver who cuts us off in rush hour traffic; the children who fail to do their chores on time; friends who are always late to our dinner dates; partners who do not do what we want them to do when we want them to do it. Alas, we cannot control other people, nor get what we want how we want it all the time. If we fail to notice that our expectations are unreasonable, we will continue to suffer.

Maybe at this point in our thinking we can see the humorous side, the silly side even, of wanting everyone around us to behave in line with our preferences all the time. Once we realize how impossible and irrational this is, we might decide to let it go.

Or maybe we can't. Maybe we absolutely cannot accept that others should not behave in line with our every rule and expectation – and so we grow more self-righteous, entitled, angry and resentful with every person's 'incorrect' behavior. This is when matters escalate. What is wrong with them? Can't they see that they need to be doing this differently? Our ego tells us that whatever we think they should do is the correct way, vindicating our anger and frustration, which will eventually reach a boiling point.

Does yelling at someone in a store improve their performance, or does it have the opposite result? We begin to see how a pattern like this, especially when it involves strong emotional reactivity on our part, interferes with our connection to others, and negatively impacts us and all those around us. By refusing to accept them, we are building a wall between ourselves and the other person. We have erected barriers to connecting in a meaningful way, creating division, and in doing so we have created a far worse kind of suffering for ourselves. This nonacceptance of others leads to our own isolation and loneliness – a real source of suffering.

The practice of acceptance is the primary antidote to this

pattern. Our challenge is to accept others, both for who they are and who they are not, without creating self-serving stories or judging and condemning them when they don't meet our expectations. Letting go of expectations as to how others should behave is the only way to knock down the walls that we build by imposing expectations on others. We recognize that everyone, ourselves included, can be annoying, difficult, and challenging at times, and that that is everyone's right – particularly since what is annoying is in the eye of the beholder. In other words, what I find annoying typically has much more to do with me than it does the person who I find annoying.

An important caveat: accepting others as they are does not mean that we have to agree with them, like them, or approve of their behavior. It does not mean we are waiving our rights or that we downplay the impact their behaviors have on us. It is not an invitation for them to abuse us, not does it deny our right to assert boundaries (that is, expectations and limitations of behavior that ensure we feel honored and respected). These are all important. Taking appropriate action and setting boundaries to protect ourselves from abuse, exploitation, or toxic behavior are signs of skillful means. We understand that clear limits must be set as required. Gotama never said that we should roll over and let people treat us badly. Our challenge is to accept the reality of who and what others are, make our peace with it in the best way we can for all involved, and move on in whatever way feels most desirable, and with integrity.

In order to achieve this, we make awareness of our inability to change others a part of our practice. We cannot afford to wait until we are in challenging interpersonal situations to try and cultivate acceptance in the heat of the moment. Our reactivity will hijack the process.

The best relationship to start with is the one we have with

ourselves – the place where our judging mind often shows up the harshest. A good way to do this is to identify a mildly challenging instance of this dynamic that doesn't carry an intense emotional charge. For instance, we may notice that we pass judgment on people as we walk by them, or that we witness highly critical thoughts arise in our mind every time we look in the mirror. Then we need to set an intention to practice accepting the person or people involved, including ourself, as they are.

For example, recently I was in line at a pharmacy to pick up a prescription. There were four people in front of me, and I needed to be somewhere else. The clerk at the counter was chit-chatting with the person at the front. I began to notice that I was tapping my foot and becoming impatient. I began to pay attention to my thoughts. 'Doesn't she know this line is long, and we're all waiting? That I am in a hurry?'. I could feel my frustration and suffering increase as I was carried along by this line of thought. But in a moment of clarity, I was able to remind myself that I had no control over her behavior. I could feel my breathing get shallow. I tensed up. I was tight. I was contracted. Even though I was in reactive mode, I recalled that I had a choice in the matter. My choice was to either act out my irritation by making loud comments about her behavior, which would have accomplished little other than causing her to become annoyed, as well as making everybody else in line uncomfortable and I would look like an entitled jerk in the process, or to just let it go.

As I noticed my bodily responses, which accompanied my self-righteous thought processes, I shifted my attention to the others in line. I intentionally slowed my breathing. I began to make small talk with the man in front of me. I made a conscious choice to let go of the expectation that the line should move faster. When I eventually made it to the counter, I remarked to the woman behind the counter that she seemed to be having a busy day, and that I hoped she was not too stressed. It was a pleasant encounter and we were all spared unnecessary suffering and embarrassment. Minor crisis averted.

In the end, my ego's sense of entitlement about the line needing to move quicker was the cause of my suffering. By mindfully paying attention to our responses, we can use everyday situations like this one as opportunities to practice acceptance when the stakes are not so high. This way, the skills are there when we really need them. Opportunities like this, where we come to a choice point about how to respond, present themselves multiple times a day. We can either go with 'snarky' entitlement, or we can practice acceptance and letting go of our attachment to how we feel others should be, recognizing that ultimately, we have no control over how they are – and when it comes to that, nor should we.

With acceptance in such situations, the whole scene softens, just as it did for me in the pharmacy. We experience a lightness of being; we experience spaciousness. Our breathing becomes relaxed, our body language becomes relaxed, our muscle tension becomes relaxed. We have a much more pleasant experience, and no one has to suffer unnecessarily, including us.

By letting go of grasping and clinging to things over which we have no control, especially in the interpersonal realm, accepting the behavior of others provides the freedom that the Buddha promised us. Instead, we open to ease, relaxation and, most importantly, to the humility that comes with acceptance. We accept that we are no more special or important than any other person in the line.

When we fail to accept people as they are, we become entangled in an unnecessary and ungraceful drama of our own making. But we can use the suffering that ensues to help us remember how good we feel when someone accepts us as we are – faults, quirks, idiosyncrasies, neuroses, and all – and choose to be one of those people too, for ourselves and for others. We soften internally and others around us relax in response.

When I went into psychotherapy as a young adult during my training, it was the first time I felt truly seen and accepted by someone, and a profound turning point in my life. It taught me that receiving such acceptance was one of the greatest gifts I could offer my psychotherapy patients. In fact, I've come to see how it is one of the greatest gifts that any person can offer another.

Being a recipient of acceptance reminds and encourages us to extend that generosity on to others by accepting them as they are. As with all generosity, acceptance is a gift that comes back to us. This is another gift of the dharma that keeps on giving: accepting others as they are, not as we wish them to be.

Reflection

✦　　How often do you find yourself wishing others would behave differently? What results do you notice when you think and feel this way? Can you recall a recent situation where practicing acceptance could have improved the outcome?

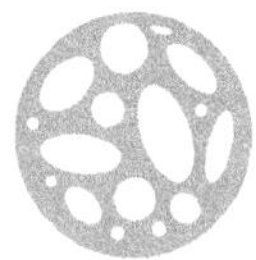

22. Regret and forgiveness

The experience of regret is actually the message; it's the lesson, the suffering that happens when we make a mistake. It's really important that we understand that, because otherwise it's like fighting ourselves. It's as though healing is taking place, but we are resisting it.

Ajahn Munindo

Simply stated, we can never completely get rid of our regrets. Our challenge is to change our relationship with them. Practical dharma has much to offer in dealing with our regrets. Regret is generally defined as a negative state, both mental and emotional, in which we engage in self-blame about the negative outcome of a past event. It typically includes a sense of loss and sorrow at what might have been, and may also include a desire to change or undo a past choice.

Regrets pervade our lives. They are like heavy weights around our ankles that we drag around. While our regrets are always with us, not far from the surface, we rarely bring them to awareness and work with them skillfully.

Who among us does not have multiple regrets – both choices made and actions taken or not taken, or opportunities lost or not taken? We spend inordinate amounts of time going over and over a regret because of our inability to let go of it. Does this not remind you of a dog chasing its tail? I've lost count of the number of regrets that I carry. Might our regrets be a function of unskillfully clinging to past actions or inactions, or trying to fix something, in the service of a wounded ego?

Before embracing the dharma I struggled with regret my whole life. Many of my regrets were focused on the parenting of my children when they were growing up. As is true for many, I had vowed to be a better parent than my parents and not repeat their mistakes. Never would I treat my children the way I had been treated. Yet I found myself repeating many of the parenting patterns with which I had been raised. I swore that I would never focus on the small stuff like clothing choices and grooming, or perfect behavior in social situations, as my mother had – the very things about which I constantly bristled as a child. Yet I repeatedly asserted control over the very same choices and behaviors being made by both of my sons when they were young. They suffered as I had. This was a primary source of my self-recrimination and regret as a parent. Only with the tools of practical dharma was I able to begin letting go of my regrets, forgiving myself for my many mistakes as a parent. As a result, and with time, I became a better parent and more forgiving of my mistakes.

Think about how we hold onto regrets. What is the point? What about the guilt and shame that accompany regret? The remorse? The sadness? The self-recrimination? What about carrying the weight of all our regrets? How it can be such a burden? We revisit our regrets repeatedly due to the mistaken belief that by doing so we can somehow fix them. This is an impossible task that serves only to cause greater suffering. What about regrets from our responses to how others treated us? Do we blame ourselves or others for how we did, or did not, respond at the time? Our regrets isolate us. We do not want to share them and feel the shame of mistakes made; we would rather hide and lick our wounds in private.

As I reflected on my relationship with the regrets in my life, it became clear that the time and energy I spent dwelling on regrets meant that I was not in the present moment. And to what end? Nothing about the past is ever changed.

We cannot be fully present and emotionally open while dwelling on regrets, clinging to them, and feeling the guilt and shame accompanying them. This only causes more suffering. Nothing is gained from regret with the exception of reminding us that we once did something we do not wish to repeat.

The first step in changing our relationship with regret is recognizing when we are entangled in them. Because we are rarely consciously aware that we are revisiting our regrets they are always lurking in the background like static that causes us to suffer – waiting to pounce and pile on with self-criticism when we do something that results in a new regret.

As with all the challenges to which we apply practical dharma, we begin by noticing our focus on regret. Without knowing what the regret is we cannot address it. To confront our regrets skillfully we begin by noticing phrases that signal regret, such as: 'if only', 'what if', 'I should have', 'I should not have', 'they should have', or 'they should not have'.

How tightly are we clinging to regrets? What, if any, function might doing so serve? Can we thoroughly examine them without judgment? Can we see regrets as one more of life's experiences that can be consciously known? I do not mean rehashing or ruminating about them. Instead, I am referring to looking at them fully and with mindful discernment and compassion, and then letting them go.

What are the thought processes that accompany our regrets? Obsessional worry? Mental images? Where are we holding regrets in our body? The stomach? Muscles of the face? Upper back? Clenched jaw?

The dharma emphasizes the importance of awareness and contact with the present moment as critical to our well-being. We can defuse (de-identify from) our regrets if the ego is heavily invested in them or if we define ourselves by them. Once we are aware that we are dwelling on regrets, we are halfway toward letting them go.

We need to use awareness to recognize regret beyond just feeling a non-specific unpleasant emotion. As I mentioned, one clue is to notice phrases that signal regret. Another indicator that we are caught in regret is an awareness that we are consumed by guilt, shame, or self-recrimination about a past action. Or we may notice that we allow our conscious and unconscious regrets to inform our self-worth.

The next step is to label it. 'This is regret' or 'this is what regret feels like'. We recognize that the behavior that led to regret was unskillful. We then respond with self-compassion and self-forgiveness, a huge part of managing regrets and letting them go.

Commonly, there is a more significant issue hiding underneath any regret. When we focus solely on the content of the regret and ruminate about it, we cannot see the larger picture. For example, regret may be driven by an underlying identification with needing to be right about a past issue or the humiliation of having lost in the face of a challenge. Both are about the ego.

We can ask if the issue about which we are feeling regret is still active in our life. If so, can we let it go? Can we set it down and lighten the load? Again, letting go means consciously choosing to challenge the regretful thought. Habits of mind can be stubborn, so we enlist self-compassion practice to help us let go of habitual thoughts that plague us. For example, we invoke phrases that we might use to comfort a close friend; or we offer self-statements of forgiveness to ourselves, reminding ourselves that we are fallible creatures for whom perfection is not attainable. We remember that we did the best we could under the circumstances at the time.

Regret is like static in our lives interfering with clarity in the present moment. Each of our lives with its unique joys and sorrows can only be lived fully by embracing the truth of our experience, including our regrets. We embrace life in all its ever-changing, impermanent, and never-perfect mystery. We do not rid ourselves of regrets, rather we change our relationship with them.

Often, letting go of regrets includes grieving past mistakes or past decisions. Doing so requires we acknowledge what was lost when we behaved in ways we regret. Did we lose the sense of ourselves as the good person we aspire to be? Did we feel diminished by losing an argument or missing an opportunity? Do we feel guilty about how we behaved or treated others? Do we regret not speaking up to someone who mistreated us or others? The list goes on and on. We are rarely without abundant opportunities for regret. Suffering ensues. Grieving a regret means facing the painful emotions accompanying the regret – leaning into the feelings and accepting the emotions. Then we can forgive ourselves, invoke self-compassion, and let go.

I have benefited from seeing regrets as teachers, when I am able to do so. Regrets are experiences from which I learned to be a better person who is more skillful in his choices and actions; a person who seeks not to repeat the same unskillful behavior going forward and who feels gratitude for the lessons learned.

Reflection

✦	Do you let your regrets define your self-worth? How would it feel to give up some of your regrets?

VII • Death and grieving

The prospect of our mortality is the three-ton elephant sitting on our chest whether we consciously acknowledge it or not – while the certainty of death is clear, the timing of our death is not; Gotama encouraged us to contemplate our death as a means of motivating us to engage fully with life.

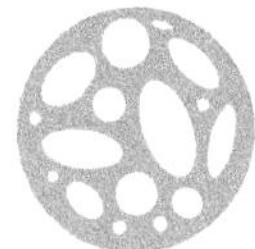

23. Facing death

It's only when we truly know and understand that we have a limited time on earth – and that we have no way of knowing when our time is up – that we will begin to live each day to the fullest, as if it was the only one we had.

Elisabeth Kubler-Ross

This book would not be complete without addressing one of life's greatest challenges: death and our mortality, something we spend so much energy denying and avoiding.

Western culture has removed death from our intimate experience. Modern medicine has set the standard that death should be prevented by any means possible. What does the dharma offer that better prepares us for this inevitable final chapter of the human experience? How does our practice support us in preparing for the loss of a loved one and the grief that follows?

Gotama taught that the mindful acknowledgment of our mortality helps us live in the present moment, appreciating every day as a precious gift. We learn to live our lives without regret so that we do not spend our last days or hours suffering about past decisions and choices made or not made. Many of the people I treated in my practice over the years had tragic deaths because they came to the end of their lives with many regrets, and the resulting guilt. A death informed by multiple regrets is not a peaceful or good death.

The ancestral Buddhist teaching about death was based on the belief system at the time that Buddhist followers borrowed from Hinduism. The teaching was that death was temporary as rebirth occurs in an endless cycle called *samsara*. The process was supposed to continue until one achieves enlightenment, called nirvana, at which point the cycle ceases.

Secular dharma does not consider metaphysical questions such as whether rebirth or reincarnation happen to be useful. These questions are unanswerable and do not bear on the daily challenges of reducing our suffering and that of those around us. We leave open the question of what happens to us after death. Instead, we focus on our relationship to the impermanence of the bodies we have in this lifetime.

Before immersing myself in Buddhist practice, I was frightened of death. I avoided thinking about it, or about situations that would remind me of it. For me, the concept of death was infused with qualities of uncertainty and a lack of control. I was preoccupied with health issues and tended toward hypochondria, imagining that I had, or would develop, every possible dreaded illness. I had no belief in an afterlife, so the finality of death was very frightening. I did not see it as a normal part of life but as an enemy of my ego and my existence, so I suffered.

With gratitude, Buddhist practice and the lessons of the dharma have helped me change my relationship with the certainty of death. I do not look forward to dying. This is because I love life, and not because of fear. I know that my endless curiosity about this life in all its beautiful complexity will someday be gone. I get so much joy from learning new things, going to new places, experiencing new adventures, and meeting new people that it saddens me to think it will end before I am done relishing life.

Having learned to let go of a high need for control, to better tolerate uncertainty and embrace impermanence, I am no longer afraid of death. I experience anticipatory grief thinking about being separated from those I love and cherish but am reassured that I will not know what it actually feels like, since I will be dead.

I have certain hopes regarding my death, of course. I intend not to leave my family with the task of cleaning up the details of my life by doing as much planning as possible. I hope not to suffer great physical pain or disability while dying. However, I accept that I have little if any control over the process of my death. Death remains on my mind frequently but more to remind me to embrace each day as a gift that brings joy, wonder, gratitude, and meaningful connections with those I love. As I watch my body age and my abilities decline, I do so with as much acceptance and gratitude for all the gifts of this life as I can muster.

Living a dharma-informed life, including all the practices we have covered, provides the means to change our relationship with death. Death is not the enemy any more than our ever-changing bodies are the enemy. Aging and death are part of the mystery of life. Indulging the fantasy that we can live forever is delusional; it is not accepting the truth of life and its finality. An essential part of changing our relationship with death is cultivating wisdom; the antithesis of holding onto the fantasy of immortality or trying to deny death.

Humankind has developed elaborate belief systems and practices over the millennia to cope with death's uncertainty and unpredictability. While such practices and beliefs may bring comfort, I believe they lack the wisdom that requires that we accept things as they are with all the uncertainty – not as our imagination with its wishful thinking tells us.

A powerful Buddhist practice thought to have been developed by Gotama is known as the five recollections. They are a 'cold water in our face' set of reminders about the impermanence of our mortality. While they may seem negative and depressing upon first reading, they can motivate us to live fully every day and take nothing for granted. The recollections are:

- **✦ I am of the nature to grow old, there is no way to escape growing old;**

- **✦ I am of the nature to have ill health, there is no way to escape having ill health;**

- **✦ I am of the nature to die, there is no way to escape death;**

- **✦ All that is dear to me and everyone I love are of the nature to change – there is no way to escape being separated from them;**

- **✦ My deeds are my closest companions, I am the beneficiary of my deeds and deeds are the ground on which I stand.**

Including the five recollections in our daily practice, may initially be difficult or upsetting. It will though, over time, help shift our relationship to our mortality and that of those we love. We might think of them as an exercise in graduated exposure for any fears of death from which we suffer.

Death is not something strange or unusual. It is happening every second all over the world. Accepting the inevitability of death supports our leading a meaningful life because there is more spaciousness in our daily lives. We are not contracting emotionally from a fear of death. The ego flails against the reality of our mortality because it cannot comprehend a time when it no longer exists.

We cling to the idea of a permanent immortal self – an exercise in futility – and we suffer as a consequence. Ironically, embracing the certainty of death, whenever and however it happens, is a source of freedom.

Reflection

✦　　Rather than avoiding thinking about death are you willing to use awareness of your own mortality to appreciate every day?

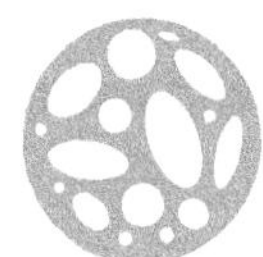

24. Grief and acceptance

To spare oneself from grief at all cost can be achieved only at the price of total detachment, which excludes the ability to experience happiness.

Erich Fromm

Regardless of who we are or the life that we have lived, grief and loss due to the death of a loved one will touch us. Because we are relational beings from our first breath we will be greatly impacted by loss. Our capacity for love, which affirms our interconnectedness, makes our experiences of loss profound. The deeper the connection the more profound the loss. The following story illustrates this truth very powerfully and is one of my favorite parables from ancient Buddhist writings, the Parable of the Mustard Seed.

During the Buddha's time, a young woman from a wealthy family was happily married to a man in her village. She had a son who became ill and died when he was a year old. Her grief was overwhelming. She could not bear the weight of it. She carried the dead child in her arms wailing and weeping

> throughout the village. She begged her friends and neighbors to help her bring her son back to life. No one was able to help her or offer her relief. Nevertheless, she persisted and begged for help all over the village.
>
> One of her neighbors was a follower of the Buddha and suggested that the young woman visit the Buddha and ask him for help. She took the dead child to the Buddha and told him of her loss and her grief. The Buddha responded to her loss with empathy, patience, and compassion. He told her: 'There is a way to solve your problem. Go to each house in the village and obtain a mustard seed from any family that has not experienced death and bring them to me.'
>
> The young woman left hopeful that the Buddha had offered a solution to her loss. She immediately began visiting every house in the village. But she soon discovered that each family she visited had experienced one or more losses from death and could not give her a mustard seed. She then realized that death comes to all families and is inevitable.
>
> With that, she was able to bury her child and give up hope of his returning to life. She understood that death is part of the experience of life and that no one is spared loss and grief.

For more than seven years, I have volunteered to facilitate bereavement groups at a local hospice organization for those who have lost a child and are grieving the loss. It is very powerful, if difficult, work. My biggest challenge is convincing the group members to accept their grief in its many forms – not fight it, not pathologize it, not feel ashamed of it, not deny it, not push it away, or minimize it. The heart-opening, however painful, is impressive to see as group members fully embrace their loss and share their feelings openly with the other group members. It is why I find the work so satisfying and why the members find it so healing. Grief is one human experience that should never be done alone. As one group member said recently, 'this is not a club I ever wanted to belong to, but I am so thankful that it exists'.

Grieving a loss can be a very lonely and isolating experience, as the parable of the mustard seed suggests. Unfortunately, most of the people who do not deal with a loss are often uncomfortable with, and avoid engaging with, someone in the throes of grief. Group members often complain about how comments from others, such as 'she's in a better place', can be unhelpful. Seeing the group members care for and support one another reinforces why we need connection and community when we struggle with life's most significant challenges.

For those dealing with the profound sorrow of losing a loved one, particularly a child, there is no substitute for sharing that grief with fellow travelers. Relationships and connection are very beneficial for someone experiencing the pain of grief. Accessing the tools of practical dharma, especially the acceptance of impermanence, supports and eases the grieving process.

People also grieve when they are dying. In coming to terms with my eventual death I alluded to the sadness that I anticipate if I know my death is imminent – not only the losses suffered by dying but also the losses due to being seriously ill. I anticipate sadness at losing my facilities and opportunities to do the things I love if I am sick. My death will cause sorrow for my loved ones, a sorrow that I am helpless to spare them. My challenge is to let go and be fully present with the truth of what is happening.

Dying people often speak of the profound sense of presence they experience as death approaches and the wisdom and clarity they achieve. They lament that they did not experience such benefits earlier in life. Is this not another argument for following a path that offers such benefits? Loss is inevitable so why not use it as a catalyst for spiritual growth and to reduce our suffering, to add perspective and spaciousness to the journey that is this life?

Sadly, in the west we have sanitized death and dying, and eliminated many of the grieving rituals that brought our ancestors together in shared grief. There is often a rush to complete a memorial service and funeral so everyone can return to their busy lives. Members of my bereavement groups complain that after the last covered dish is eaten, they feel alone and without support from anyone who understands their pain. The task of settling an estate and tying up loose ends in the deceased's life can be overwhelming and add additional stress to the experience of loss. Ideally, someone's community can be a helpful resource in navigating the maze of details.

As with much that we emphasize in practical dharma, the practice of acceptance is primary though it is no panacea for the pain of loss. Spiritual practice cannot help us avoid the pain of grief. Yet, by employing the tools available to us the loss can be held with greater compassion, perspective, and spaciousness.

Acceptance takes both time and actively facing loss. Though grief comes in strong waves we welcome it as necessary and unavoidable. Someone I know, who recently lost a child, told me that something was wrong with her because she could not stop crying. She insisted that she needed to stop crying. I responded that she needed to cry more and not try to stop as the grief needed to be accepted, as painful as it was, and faced openly. Repressing it would only prolong the grief.

I could not adequately grieve my father's death until I let go of many residual emotions and face my loss clearly without the confusion of strong feelings. When he was alive there was too much noise in the system in the form of unresolved emotions for me to gain clarity about my complicated feelings toward him. When he died, I deeply grieved not only his death but also the missed opportunities during his lifetime for a deeper connection with him – the result of my holding onto unrealistic expectations.

Grief is real, it is raw, and it is painful – but it is also heart-opening like nothing else I have experienced. There are no shortcuts to grieving; we must show up for it and welcome it without trying to avoid or run from it. In my experience, using the tools of secular dharma can be extremely helpful in facing our losses.

Notwithstanding the pain, I have grown emotionally and spiritually from every major loss I have suffered. Some of my most profound losses have been the death of pets – I often joke that I grieve more deeply over the death of one of my beloved dogs than I ever have for a person.

The heart opening and the development of compassion for myself and others, as well as the wisdom gained, could only have come from experiencing loss. Every significant experience in our lives, loss included, is an opportunity to either learn and grow as opposed to withdrawing, avoiding, and hiding.

Accepting impermanence while seeing suffering as a teacher and embracing the sorrow in our lives are not inborn dispositions. They must be cultivated and acquired. The dharma makes that possible – with the effort comes the promise of liberation and emotional freedom.

Reflection

✦   Think about where in your life you have experienced grief. Did you accept your grief and face it or try to avoid it by distracting yourself?

Afterword

I know no better example of the transformative power of Buddhist practice than my own life. Since I started on this path, I have gone from being a driven, impatient, anxious, unhappy, angry and controlling workaholic who made those around him miserable, to someone who sees life more clearly, with greater joy and spaciousness. I feel more deeply connected to those I love, and see joy and wonder in the natural world. My reactivity has dramatically decreased as I now take more things in stride. I try not to control those things which I cannot control, and more readily let go of irritation and frustration. I am grateful for the gift of each day and all that it offers.

My life remains full of challenges and contradictions. I still get hooked by grasping and clinging to things that I know to be impermanent. Nonetheless, I am grateful for the gifts of both ancient wisdom and modern psychology, which have been roadmaps on my journey. My gratitude has spread to include the many other gifts of this life. I no longer take any of the blessings for granted. I acknowledge with gratitude how fortunate I am to have all the experiences of this difficult and joyful life.

I am not a misty-eyed Pollyanna. Long-term habits of the mind are not easy to challenge. When teaching, I say that if these practices can be transformative for me, they can be life-changing for anyone. During the years I was unhappy and feeling lost, I was unable to imagine a way out of the darkness. As the methods described in this book have brought me into the light of awareness and joy, I greet each day with gratitude.

To help you begin finding more joy in your own life I leave you with a few reminders and takeaways.

+ The essential and common threads through all the topics we covered include noticing, pausing, and discernment. These require mindfulness, present-moment awareness, intention, and patience. They are essential to the path and must be practiced daily. This is not an easy practice and we will not succeed if we are operating on autopilot.

+ Be mindful of the ways we get tripped up on our journey. The three poisons of greed, hatred, and delusion explain most of where and how we suffer, and cause suffering to others. Subsumed under these challenges are the denial of impermanence, the ego's siren call ('I', 'me', 'mine'), the reactivity we act out, as well as the shame and avoidance we experience.

+ Relationships, and our actions within them and in response and reactivity to them, make us human and are central to our existence. It is difficult to see our suffering without the mirroring of others. We do poorly when we are alone and isolated, both of which are sources of tremendous suffering. Successful relationships require work and sacrifice and are never easy; they require acceptance that the best of them is imperfect. Yet the rewards are without parallel.

✦ The positive practices of the four immeasurables (loving kindness, equanimity, compassion, and sympathetic joy), the ten perfections, gratitude practice, and cultivating joy are antidotes to the toxic emotions, attitudes, and behaviors that we addressed. Without making these aspects of the teachings a part of our daily lives we will not change. 'Wishing won't make it so', as the saying goes. They need to be an integral part of our daily practice.

✦ As has been true in my life, the eightfold path attracts those who want to find healing from their past experiences. The eightfold path serves as a starting point for personal development yet it does not represent the final stage of growth. Through the eightfold path we learn to connect with others by showing generosity while using our wisdom and love to guide our actions. Our personal liberation from suffering enables us to establish conditions which help others achieve their own liberation. May we walk this path together, with courage, clarity, and love.

I hope you found this book helpful and supportive and that it resonated with your struggles. Additional volumes could be, and have been, written about other aspects of secular Buddhism and Buddhist practices as well as modern psychology. I have tried to present a brief but accessible overview of the most effective and achievable practices from each to reduce our suffering and improve the quality of our busy lives.

Gotama told his listeners not to take for granted anything he taught. Instead, he told them to follow his teachings and see if they worked. I encourage you to do the same with secular dharma. Do not take my word for anything. Trust your own direct experiences as you experiment and observe what reduces your suffering. Start your journey on the path now, find a face-to-face or virtual community, start a meditation practice, study the teachings, and see for yourself. Doing so will cost you nothing but time and effort, and the reward will be a richer and more joyful life filled with compassion and gratitude for all your experiences. I wish you many blessings in your life's journey. Peace to you and yours.

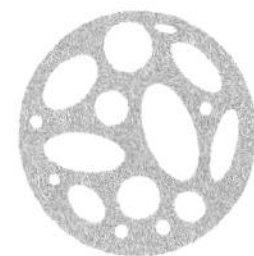

About the author

Now retired, Jeffrey Fracher was in practice for 44 years as a clinical psychologist in New Jersey and Virginia. He has practiced Buddhism since 1992 when he committed to the Buddhist path by taking lay precepts in the sangha of the late Thich Nhat Hanh.

In 2013 he completed a two-year Buddhist teacher training program at the Meditation Teachers Training Institute in Washington DC. He was a senior teacher at the Insight Meditation Community of Charlottesville for ten years, where he was also president of the Board of Directors, retiring in 2022.

At the request of his students, he then founded Serenity Sangha, a far-reaching virtual and face-to-face community of Buddhist practitioners which emphasizes practical dharma, a synthesis of modern psychology and secular Buddhist wisdom.

A native Virginian, Jeff lives in Charlottesville, VA, with his wife of 53 years, Kay, and his two beloved rescued golden retrievers, Kaiya and Khema. He has two adult sons, Eli and Luke. In addition to leading Serenity Sangha, he is a Clinical Assistant Professor in the Clinical Psychology PhD program at the University of Virginia, and a volunteer bereavement group facilitator at the Hospice of the Piedmont. He also serves as chair of the City of Charlottesville

Police Civilian Oversight Board, and is the founder and chair of the Charlottesville Parks Foundation.

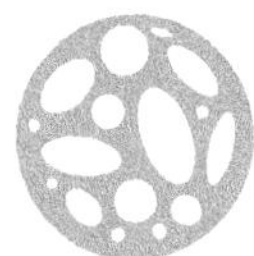

Acknowledgements

The list of people to whom I am grateful for help and support with this project is quite long. Nevertheless, I apologize to those I may have overlooked and failed to mention.

First and foremost, my deep gratitude to my beloved Kay. What began as an 8th grade crush many years ago, evolved into one of the great joys of my life. Her support and love through all my life challenges, including this project, are immeasurable.

The members of Serenity Sangha, who encouraged me to commit my teachings to paper, inspired this project. Their commitment to the path of practical dharma inspires me every day and brings me great joy.

Much gratitude for my personal teacher of many years, Lila Kate Wheeler, who has guided me, confronted me, supported me, believed in me, and helped me become a better person. She is a repository of great dharma wisdom and she has most generously shared it with me.

Admiration and gratitude to Tuwhiri's editorial board – Cathryn Jacob, Ramsey Margolis and Winton Higgins – for their support and willingness to bring this project to fruition.

Finally, to all the teachers, therapists, mentors, supervisors, role models, friends, colleagues, pets, adversaries, psychotherapy patients and family members, who have taught me, challenged me, supported me, and guided me on my life's journey. Thank you.

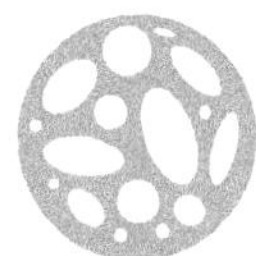

Sources of wisdom

Here are some books and articles which have guided and informed my secular Buddhist path, and which I recommend.

American Bible Society. (1995) *The Holy Bible: Contemporary English version.*

Anderson, B. (2019) *The Buddha's Guide to Gratitude: The Life-Changing Power of Everyday Mindfulness.* IMango Publishing.

Armstrong, K. (2001) *Buddha: A Penguin Life.* Lipper/Viking.

Batchelor, S. (1997) *Buddhism without Beliefs: A Contemporary Guide to Awakening.* Riverhead Books.

Batchelor, S. (2011) *Confession of a Buddhist Atheist.* Random House.

Batchelor, S. (2015) *The Faith to Doubt.* Counterpoint.

Batchelor, S. (2017) *After Buddhism.* Yale University Press.

Batchelor, S. (2018) *Secular Buddhism.* Yale University Press.

Batchelor, S. (2019) *Alone with Others.* Grove Press.

Batchelor, S. (2022) *The Art of Solitude.* Yale University Press.

Batchelor, S. (2025) *Buddha, Socrates, and Us.* Yale University Press

Bernstein, W.J. (2021) *The Delusions of Crowds: Why People Go Mad in Groups.* Atlantic Monthly Press.

Bodhi, B. (2000) *The Noble Eightfold Path: Way to the End of Suffering.* BPS Pariyatti Editions.

Bodhi, B. (2015) *In the Buddha's Words: An Anthology of Discourses from the Pali Canon.* Wisdom Publications.

Brady, M. (2003) *The Wisdom of Listening.* Wisdom Publications.

Brahma Viharas. Four Immeasurables. (2015, January 27) Retrieved September 4, 2022, from https://brahmaviharas.net.

The Dhammapada: The Buddha's Path of Wisdom. (1996) Buddhist Publication Society.

Buswell, R.E., & Lopez, D.S. (2014) *The Princeton Dictionary of Buddhism.* Princeton University Press.

Chodron, P. (1998) *When Things Fall Apart.* Shambhala.

Dalai Lama & Tutu, D. (2016) *The Book of Joy: Lasting Happiness in a Changing World.* Avery Penguin Random House.

Dalai Lama. (2007) *How to See Yourself as You Really Are.* Atria Press.

Dessen, S. (2013) *What Happened to Goodbye.* Speak Press

Dhammapala, A., & Bodhi, B. (1996) *A Treatise on the Paramis: From the Commentary to the Cariyapitaka.* Buddhist Publication Society.

Epstein, M. (1999) *Going to Pieces Without Falling Apart: A Buddhist Perspective on Wholeness.* Broadway Books.

Epstein, M. (2018) *Advice Not Given: A Guide to Getting Over Yourself.* Penguin Press.

Feldman, C. (2017) *Boundless Heart: The Buddha's Path of Kindness, Compassion, Joy, and Equanimity.* Shambhala Publications, Inc.

Fronsdal, G. (2006) *The Dhammapada: A New Translation of the Buddhist Classic with Annotations.* Shambhala Publications, Inc.

Fronsdal, G. (2008) *The Issue at Hand: Essays on Buddhist Mindfulness Practice.* Insight Meditation Center.

Fromm, E. (1947) *Man for Himself: An Inquiry Into the Psychology of Ethics.* Rinehart.

Fundamentals of Buddhism: Wisdom. (n.d.) Retrieved September 4, 2022, from https://www.buddhanet.net/fundbud8.htm.

Germer, C.K. (2009) *The Mindful Path to Self-Compassion: Freeing Yourself From Destructive Thoughts and Emotions.* Guilford Press.

Gleig, A. (2019) *American Dharma: Buddhism Beyond Modernity.* Yale University Press.

Goldstein, J. (2016) *Mindfulness: A Practical Guide to Awakening.* Sounds True.

Goleman, D. (2004) *Destructive Emotions: How Can We Overcome Them? A Scientific Dialogue with the Dalai Lama.* Bantam Books.

Gunaratana, H. (1992) *Mindfulness in Plain English.* Wisdom Publications.

Hanh T.N. & Kotler, A. (1996) *Being Peace.* Parallax Press.

Hanh T.N. & Laity, A. (1993) *The Blooming of a Lotus: Guided Miracle of Mindfulness.* Beacon Press.

Hanh T.N. (1998) *Old Path, White Clouds: Walking in the Footsteps of the Buddha.* Full Circle.

Hanson, R. (2020) *Neurodharma.* Harmony Books.

Hanson, R. & Mendius, R. (2009) *Buddha's Brain: The Practical Neuroscience of Happiness, Love & Wisdom.* New Harbinger Publications.

Harari, Y. N. (2018) *Sapiens: A Brief History of Humankind.* Harper Perennial.

Harris, R. (2012) *The Reality Slap.* New Harbinger Publications.

Hartley, B.L. (2024) *No Nonsense Spirituality.* SacraSage Publications.

Hayes, S.C. (2005) *Get Out of Your Mind & Into Your Life.* New Harbinger Publications.

Hesse, H. (1910) *Gertrude.* Picador Press.

Higgins, W. (2021) *Revamp: Writings on Secular Buddhism.* Tuwhiri.

Jung, C.G., & Hinkle, B.M. (2003) *Psychology of the Unconscious.* Dover Publications.

Junger, S. (2017) *Tribe: On Homecoming and Belonging.* 4th Estate.

Kabat-Zinn, J. (1994) *Wherever You Go, There You Are: Mindfulness Meditation in Everyday Life.* Hyperion.

Kubler-Ross, E. (1959) *On Death and Dying.* Macmillan.

Kyokai, B.D. (1997) *The Teaching of Buddha.* Japan Publications.

Ladner, L. (2004) *The Lost Art of Compassion: Discovering the Practice of Happiness in the Meeting of Buddhism and Psychology.* Harper San Francisco.

Lao-Tzu (1990) *Tao Te Ching.* Kyle Cathie, Ltd.

Metamorphosis. (2021) *The Mustard Seed of Grief and Rebirth.* Buddhistdoor Global. Retrieved September 4, 2022, from https://www.buddhistdoor. net/features/the-mustard-seed-of-grief-and-rebirth.

Moffitt, P. (2008) *Dancing with Life: Finding Meaning and Joy in the Face of Suffering.* Rodale.

Moffitt, P. (2012) *Emotional Chaos to Clarity: How to Live More Skillfully, Make Better Decisions, and Find Purpose in Life.* Hudson Street Press.

Müller, F.M., & Maguire, J. (2002) *Dhammapada: Annotated & Explained.* SkyLight Paths Pub.

Munindo, A. (1995) Regret and Well Being. Retrieved September 4, 2022. from https://www.budsas.org/ebud/ebdha029.htm.

Nathanson, D.L. (1987) *The Many Faces of Shame.* Guilford Press.

Nathanson, D.L. (1992) *Shame and Pride: Affect, Sex, and the Birth of the Self.* Norton.

Nyanaponika. (1993) *The Five Mental Hindrances and Their Conquest: Selected Texts from the Pali Canon and the Commentaries.* Buddhist

Publication Society.

O'Brien, B. (2018) *The Three Poisons – in Buddhism, the Roots of Unhappiness.* Learn Religions. Retrieved September 4, 2022, from https://www.learnreligions.com/the-three-poisons-449603.

Palmo, J.T. (2011) *Into the Heart of Life.* Snow Lion Publications.

Pasha, R. (2020, April 13) *67 Famous Theodore Roosevelt Quotes.* Retrieved September 4, 2022, from https://succeedfeed.com/theodore-roosevelt-quotes.

Richards, V. & Wilce, G. (1996) *The Person Who Is Me: Contemporary Perspectives on the True and False Self.* Karnac Books.

Rothberg, D. (2006) *The Engaged Spiritual Life: A Buddhist Approach to Transforming Ourselves and the World.* Beacon Press.

Rumi J. al-D. & Barks, C. (2004) *The Essential Rumi.* HarperCollins.

Smedes, L.B. (1997) *The Art of Forgiving: When You Need to Forgive and Don't Know How.* Ballantine Books.

Staff, L.R. (2019, December 6) *What are the Five Recollections? Retrieved September 4, 2022, from https://www.lionsroar.com/buddhism-by-the-numbers-the-five-recollections.*

Thera, Ñ. (1960-65) Notes on Dhamma. Pathpress Publications.

Treleaven, D.A. & Britton, W. (2018) *Trauma-Sensitive Mindfulness: Practices for Safe and Transformative Healing.* W.W Norton & Company.

Watts, A. (1957) *The Way of Zen.* Random House Vintage Books.

Wikimedia Foundation. (2022, August 27) *Buddhist Ethics.* Wikipedia. Retrieved September 4, 2022, from https://en.wikipedia.org/wiki/Buddhist_ethics.

Wilde, O. (2014) *Oscar Wilde, Complete Collection.* CreateSpace Independent Publishing Platform.

Working with the Hard Stuff: Courage to Open to the Whole Show. (2019, August 31) *https://awakeningjoy.info/blog/working-with-the-hard-stuff-courage-to-open-to-the-whole-show.*

Yoda, M. (1999) *The Phantom Menace.* Retrieved September 4, 2022, from https://starwars.com/news/the-starwars-com-10-best-yoda-quotes.

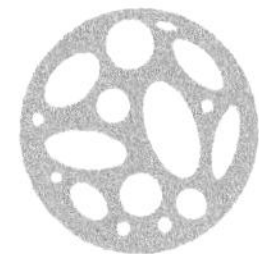

Index

A

acceptance
  as attitude, 24, 117
  as practice, 20, 22, 161
  for psychological flexibility, 23
  in relationships, 66–67, 140,
    155, 157, 159–60, 162
  of aging, 173
  of loss and grief, 25, 145, 177,
    179–81
  of suffering and
    impermanence, 21, 97, 118
  through mindfulness, 116
action, 104–06
  Actualize a path, xii
addictions, 43
  compulsive, 45–46
afterlife, 172
aging, 173
amygdala, 61–62
anger
  cultivating patience and
    forgiveness, 53
  in relationships, 51
  mindfulness practices for, 52
  reactive emotion, 49–50
anxiety
  causes and conditions of, 22,
    55–56
    cessation and non-
      attachment to, 23
    craving and reactivity in, 59
    daily-life practices for, 57, 62
    mindfulness-based
      acceptance of, 58, 60–61,
      63
Aotearoa Buddhist Education Trust,
  v
Aotearoa New Zealand, v
attachment, 125–27
autonomy, 148–49, 151
aversion, 13–14
awakening, 117–18, 152
  See also enlightenment
awareness
  as discernment, 16
  discernment
    distinguishing skillful
      from unskillful, 127
    for ethical living, 67, 151
    for regulating reactivity,
      70, 88, 95, 138
    in cessation of craving,
      46, 89
    in daily life, 68–69, 148
    in mindfulness practice,
      110
  for compassion, 52, 157

for ethical action, 101, 103, 105–06
in daily life, xii, xv, 116, 139
in experiencing life fully, 1, 118
nonjudgmental stance, 135
noticing
  interrupting reactivity, 92–95
  of craving and cessation, 88
  of habitual patterns, 89
of craving, xiv
of impermanence, 60
of suffering, 17
present-moment practice, 55, 107

B
Batchelor, Stephen
  eightfold path and four noble truths, xv
  evidence-based approach, x, 5, 7
  secular reinterpretation of Buddhism, xi–xii
beginner's mind, 123
bereavement groups, 178
boundaries
  autonomy and self-care, 150
  in relationships, 147–49, 151, 159
breath, 97, 111
Buddhist ethics
  four immeasurables, 74, 82–83, 185
  integration with mindfulness and psychology, 105–06
  intention and motivation in, 104
  non-harm and responsible action, 102
  secular foundations of, 101
Buddhist philosophy, 115
  mindfulness, foundations of, 83, 109

Buddhist teachings, 31
  eightfold path, xv, 6, 70, 104, 108, 112, 151, 185
  four noble truths, x
  four tasks, x–xii

C
cause, 93
cerebral cortex, 52, 55
cessation, xv
  See also See reactivity stop
choices, 96
clarity, 93
claustrophobia, 62
cognitive defusion, 83
communication, 104
  speech, 105
community, 4, 7, 179–80
  Sangha, Serenity, vi
compassion
  and emotional regulation, 52, 67, 97, 180
  and reactivity, 40, 42, 66, 68, 135
  as experiential learning, 117–18, 181
  for others, 140
  for self, 11, 74, 110, 143, 145, 150
  in daily life, xv, 1, 116
  in ethical living, 102–03, 151–52
  secular framing of, 101
competition, 72, 75
connection
  countering reactivity, 75
  in grief and loss, 177, 179
  in relationships, 133–35, 140
  intimacy, 136–38, 140
  through community engagement, 143
  with oneself, 141
contentment, 8, 121, 123
coping, 96
  avoidance
    letting go of reactivity, 95

maladaptive coping, 44,
46, 88, 91, 94, 96
reinforcing suffering,
20–22
core values, 36
craving
as cause of suffering, xii, 13,
15, 17, 43, 88
bodily sensations of, 44–45
in cycle of reactivity, xiii, 40
recognizing cessation of, xiv,
16

D
death
as motivation for living fully,
169, 171, 174
grief and acceptance, 173
impermanence and, 175
in secular Buddhism, 172
desire
as experiential avoidance, 43,
46, 88
for sense pleasures and
validation, 44
mindfulness and letting go,
45, 47, 89
dharma
cessation of craving, 128
community engagement, 179
compassion and kindness,
52, 145
daily life applications, 8, 86,
121, 134, 151, 171
discernment and wisdom, 46,
140
emotional regulation, 71, 96,
163, 165
ethical duty, 142
ethics, 4, 7
flexibility of path, 1
healing emotional wounds, 11,
51, 59, 81, 144, 148, 162
human flourishing, 12, 84, 115,
118
in Buddhist and Jain

traditions, 178
middle way, 6, 152
mindfulness practices, 68, 122
personal testing of teachings,
117, 130
philosophical foundations,
172
practical methodology, 116,
120
psychological framing, 72, 74
reactivity and craving, 5, 14,
41, 44, 47, 70, 77, 92
relational harmony, 83, 131,
133, 149
resilience building, 69, 80, 98
secular reinterpretation of, 4,
79, 146, 176
suffering and impermanence,
10, 15, 58, 82, 135, 169, 173
without supernatural beliefs,
56
doubt, 129–30
dysfunction, 136–37

E
effect, 93
karma, 87
ego
as mental construct, 28
compassion and detachment
for, 30, 84
craving and attachment, 19,
161, 164
driver of suffering, 32, 72, 135
false self, 30–31
mindfulness for recognizing,
74, 166
overidentification with, 27
pride, 28–29, 49–51, 72
reactivity from, 29, 37, 39, 51,
53, 75, 86, 158
resistance to impermanence,
68–69, 156
self-identity, 27, 29, 31, 147
emotional reactivity
cessation and non-

attachment, xiv
    ego patterns and identity, 29,
       158
    ethical practice and conduct,
       53
    from attachment and shame,
       35, 38–39, 89
    in relationships, 137, 139
    in the four tasks, xi–xiii
    mindfulness practices for, 41,
       94, 183
    roots in craving and aversion,
       33, 37, 49–50
    self-compassion for, 40, 42, 92
empathy, 135, 140, 142–43
enlightenment, 172
    See also awakening
    nirvana, 172
envy, 74–75
ethical foundation, 112–13
    livelihood, 105
executive function, 29
    emotional regulation, 42, 97
experience, 12–15
    Experience life, xii–xiii
exposure, 56–57, 61–62

F
faith, 128–30
    confirmed faith, 128–29
fear, 56–57
fear of missing out (FOMO), 71
fight, 93–95
    See also flight
five hindrances, 109
five precepts, 102
flight, 94–95
    See also fight
flourishing, 119
forgiveness, 52–53, 66, 167
Fracher, Jeffrey C, iv
freedom, 16, 23
    spiritual freedom, 152
freeze response, 61, 94

G
generosity, 82, 84, 123
Gotama
    applicability to daily life, 58,
       119, 169, 171
    as historical human teacher, 5
    Batchelor's four tasks from,
       109
    experiential testing of
       teachings, 11, 118, 129, 185
    integration with modern
       psychology, 84, 116
    on cessation of craving, 17
    on craving, reactivity, and
       letting go, 15–16, 38
    on ethical living and
       compassion, 112–13, 177–78
    on mindfulness practice, 59,
       108
    on non-attachment and
       freedom, 27, 161
    practical methods for well-
       being, 6
    rejection of supernatural
       claims, 56
    secular reinterpretations of,
       79
    teachings on suffering and
       impermanence, 9, 12, 19
grasping, 20, 136, 144, 161
gratitude
    and impermanence, 172–73
    cultivating compassion and
       generosity, 121, 123
    present-moment practice,
       122, 124
guilt
    from unskillful actions, 37
    reactivity and clinging in,
       164–65
    self-compassion and
       forgiveness for, 166–67

H
Hanh, Thich Nhat, 3, 7, 12
hope, 128–30
    See also wise hope
hospice, 178
humor, 139

I
ill will
    arising from anger and
        reactivity, 49–50, 53
    effects on relationships and
        mindfulness, 51–52
    hostility, 50–51
    resentment, 50, 156
impatience
    cultivating patience and
        acceptance, 67, 69
    reactivity and negative
        emotions, 65–66, 70
    roots in attachment and
        expectations, 68
impermanence
    and craving, 15, 20, 73
    and non-attachment, 16, 134
    and suffering, 9, 19, 21, 82
    for resilience, 57, 81, 91, 126–27
    in daily life, 25, 124, 173, 179
    in mindfulness practice, 60
    in reducing reactivity, 13–14,
        23
    in secular Buddhism, 172
    openness and curiosity
        toward, 24, 133, 135
intention, 104, 106
isolation, 51, 158

J
joy, 79, 121–23
judgment
    as cognitive function, 72–73
    comparison, 71–72
    in craving and reactivity, 68,
        89
    self-criticism, 72, 163–64, 166
    self-judgment, 71, 157

    softening through
        mindfulness, 74
Jung, Carl, 89

L
letting go
    for emotional regulation, 161,
        165
    of control and expectations,
        140, 145, 159, 167
    with self-compassion, 160,
        164, 166
loss, 180–81
    grief, 171, 177–81

M
meditation
    cessation of craving, 109
    compassion and wisdom, 113
    ethical living, 112
    in daily life, 1, 186
    reactivity management, 58,
        94, 107–08, 110–11
    suffering and impermanence,
        10, 97
modern psychology, 84, 183, 185
Munindo, Ajahn, 163
muscle memory, 94
Mustard Seed, Parable of the, 177,
179

N
neocortex, 61
neuroscience, 7, 61, 84
no fixed self, 83
non-grasping, xiv
non-harming, 7
non-reactivity, 66

O
overwhelm
    cultivating a mindful path, 98
    letting go of reactivity, 92–93,
        95–97

P
patience
    and letting go of reactivity,
       66, 70
    for navigating impermanence,
       68
    in compassionate response,
       67
    on the mindful path, 65, 69
peer pressure, 73
practice, 128–30, 171
psychology
    evidence-based methods, 8
    integration with secular
       Buddhism, 7, 9, 116, 118
    psychological flexibility,
       36–37, 42
    psychological pain, 21
    psychotherapy, 62, 162
    resilience and behavior
       change, 117

R
rebirth, 172
regret
    acceptance and letting go, 163
    as barrier to presence, 165,
       167
    clinging and ego
       identification, 164
    in the body, 166
relationships
    boundaries in, 147–49, 151–52
    conflict and suffering in, 131,
       135, 184
    emotional regulation in, 150
    impermanence of, 133, 155
    in community life, 134
renunciation, 46
resilience, 123
restraint, 46
revenge, 49

S
Salzberg, Sharon, 128–29
secular Buddhism
    Batchelor's four tasks, xi
    discernment, 102

    embracing suffering, 11, 79
    emotional regulation, 86
    experiential learning, 185
    impermanence and change, 9
    integration with psychology,
       32, 84
    managing reactivity, 14
    non-attachment, 125
    personal responsibility, 112
    sanghas, 7
    Secular Buddhist Association,
       v
    Secular Buddhist Book
       Project, v
    self-compassion, 181
    well-being and flourishing,
       iii–iv, 12, 76, 78, 100
    woundedness and healing, 31
See reactivity stop, xii, xiv
    See also cessation
self-awareness, 36, 109
self-compassion
    emotion regulation and
       reactivity, 40, 42
    for shame and self-criticism,
       30–31, 166–67
    recognizing impermanence,
       60
self-forgiveness, 30
shadow side, 30, 89
shame
    defensive behaviors to avoid,
       35, 49, 51
    ego and self-image, 28, 39
    fear of judgment and
       rejection, 29, 38, 72–73
    mindful awareness of, 37
    self-compassion for, 30, 40,
       42, 166–67
    self-criticism and hiding,
       164–65
skillful responding, 99
    wise speech, 138
social media, 68, 71
    influencers, 73
status, 72–75
suffering

aging, loss, and death, 22, 173, 180

attachment and aversion, 125, 135, 143, 156

community engagement around, 12, 118

craving as driver, 13, 15, 17

emotional wounds, 134, 141, 145

ethical responses to, 149–50

impermanence, 9, 19–21, 172, 181

letting go of reactivity, xiii, 14, 77, 144, 159–60

mindfulness for acceptance, 6, 16, 23, 116–17, 161

moments of freedom from, 7

motivation for practice, xi–xii, 10, 32, 69, 79, 126

non-attachment and discernment, 68, 127, 147–48

openness and curiosity toward, 158

reactivity cycles, 33, 70–71

responding to others' suffering, 140, 151

secular interpretation of, 5, 11

self-compassion for, 167

shame and regret, 35, 157, 163–65

universal condition, 3

supernatural, 79
sympathetic joy, 74
sympathetic nervous system, 97

T
ten perfections, 185
three poisons, 29, 184
trauma, 30–31
trust, 137, 139, 147
Tuwhiri, v

U
uncertainty, 21

V
violence, 50
virtue, 65

equanimity

amid impermanence and uncertainty, 82, 84, 97

reducing reactivity, 36–37, 49–50, 83

supporting compassion and patience, 65, 67, 70, 75, 123

vulnerability, 140

W
well-being

ethical living, 101, 103, 118

in secular Buddhism, 12, 78, 100

mindfulness for acceptance, 14, 116

psychological aspects, 76

setting boundaries, 147

wisdom and insight, 102

Winnicott, D. W., 30
wisdom

Buddhist wisdom, x

for ethical discernment, 102, 140

in cessation of craving, 17

in community engagement, 4

in daily life, xii, xv, 1, 101, 152

in emotional regulation and resilience, 183

in letting go of reactivity, xiii, 6

recognizing impermanence and suffering, 19, 173, 181

wise hope, 125–27

See also hope

wonder, 121–23

awe, 123

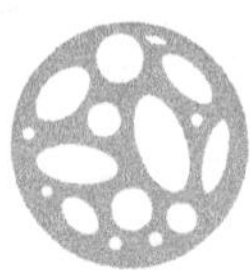

Taking the next step

The talks brought together in the production of this book were given by Jeff Fracher during meetings of Serenity Sangha.

Are you interested in pursuing a secular path towards reducing suffering, and fully engaging with life? You'd be most welcome to drop into one of our online meetings and say 'hi'. Guided meditation instructions will be offered for those new to meditation.

Serenity Sangha is a virtual community of practitioners whose participants live not just in the United States but throughout the world. Connect with us on Zoom on Wednesday and Saturday at 10am US EST for for a teaching, discussion, and meditation. Meetings run for approximately 75 minutes.

As taught some 2400 years ago in what is now northern India by Gotama, the man we know as the Buddha, our emphasis is on practical dharma from a contemporary, secular perspective. Bringing together a secular approach to the teachings of the Buddha with modern psychology, this approach emphasises teachings which have pragmatic and accessible applications to the challenges of daily living.

For more information go to

https://serenitysangha.org/offerings

or write to

serenitysanghacville@gmail.com

and sign up for a weekly Substack newsletter at

https://jeffreyfracher.substack.com.

TUWHIRI

FINDING MEANING IN A DIFFICULT WORLD

revealing … making known …
a means of discovering something lost or hidden …
examining long-established Buddhist teachings with fresh eyes

REVAMP Writings on secular Buddhism
Winton Higgins

978-0-473-57138-2 • USD $19.95

Winton Higgins tracks the emergence of a secular Buddhism with a focus on today's climate emergency and intensifying social injustice. The ethic of care that underpins a creative dharma practice, he suggests, calls on us to bring our training to bear on these urgent tasks.

WHAT IS THIS?
Ancient questions for modern minds
Martine and Stephen Batchelor

978-9-473-47498-0 • USD $19.95

Martine and Stephen Batchelor lead us through the practice of radical questioning at the heart of this Korean Buddhist tradition. They show how anyone at all can benefit from this form of radical inquiry today.

MINDFUL SOLIDARITY
A secular Buddhist democratic socialist dialogue
Mike Slott

978-8-990-94910-2 • USD $19.95

Mike Slott encourages political activists and Buddhist practitioners to connect with and learn from each other, maintaining that we need to pursue both individual and social transformation.

LIVING LIFE ON LIFE'S TERMS
Turning the wheels of secular dharma
Stephen Batchelor, Martine Batchelor and Bernat Font

979-8-9909491-1-9 • USD $19.95

Three voices bring secular dharma to life. Stephen Batchelor offers a tapestry of philosophical insight, Martine Batchelor shares guidance for weaving practice into daily life, while Bernat Font adds creativity and warmth through stories and metaphors.

https://tuwhiri.org ❖ ask@tuwhiri.org ❖ https://tuwhiri.substack.com